CAMPAIGN 313

THE PHILIPPINE SEA 1944

The last great carrier battle

MARK STILLE

ILLUSTRATED BY JIM LAURIER
Series editor Marcus Cowper

OSPREY PUBLISHING
Bloomsbury Publishing Plc

Kemp House, Chawley Park, Cumnor Hill, Oxford OX2 9PH, UK
29 Earlsfort Terrace, Dublin 2, Ireland
1385 Broadway, 5th Floor, New York, NY 10018, USA
Email: info@ospreypublishing.com
www.ospreypublishing.com

OSPREY is a trademark of Osprey Publishing Ltd

First published in Great Britain in 2017
Transferred to digital print in 2024

A catalogue record for this book is available from the British Library

Print ISBN: 978 1 4728 1920 8
ePub: 978 1 4728 1922 2
ePDF: 978 1 4728 1921 5
XML: 978 1 4728 2377 9

Index by Fionbar Lyons
Maps by www.bounford.com
3D BEVs by The Black Spot
Typeset in Myriad Pro and Sabon
Page layouts by PDQ Digital Media Solutions, Bungay, UK
Printed and bound in Great Britain by CPI (Group) UK Ltd, Croydon CR0 4YY

24 25 26 27 28   10 9 8 7 6

The Woodland Trust
Osprey Publishing supports the Woodland Trust, the UK's leading woodland
conservation charity.

www.ospreypublishing.com
To find out more about our authors and books visit our website. Here you will
find extracts, author interviews, details of forthcoming events and the option
to sign-up for our newsletter.

CONTENTS

Strategic situation, June 1, 1944

INTRODUCTION

The battle of the Philippine Sea, fought in June 1944, has been somewhat overlooked compared to other major Pacific War naval battles. The encounter in the Philippine Sea was almost exclusively a carrier battle, the fifth of the Pacific War. As a carrier battle, it was by far the largest ever fought with 15 fleet and light carriers on the American side and nine on the Japanese side. By comparison, the second-largest carrier battle of the war, Midway, featured seven carriers. No other carrier battle of this magnitude will ever be seen again.

Even ignoring the unique carrier aspect of this battle, it was an engagement of tremendous size. The United States Navy (USN) brought some 165 combatants to the action and almost 900 aircraft on the fleet and light carriers complemented by another 170 aircraft on seven escort carriers. The Imperial Japanese Navy (IJN) mustered over 50 combatants for this battle, and just over 400 carrier-based aircraft and more than 300 land-based aircraft. For sheer size alone, the battle of the Philippine Sea was the second-largest naval engagement of the Pacific War, surpassed only by the battle of Leyte Gulf fought a few months later.

Many accounts of naval warfare in the Pacific use the term "decisive" too readily when describing the principal naval battles of the war. In the case of Philippine Sea, the term is no exaggeration. The American objective of the battle was to seize the Marianas Islands that provided air bases for the long-range bombardment of Japan. The USN expected a major reaction from the IJN, so the destruction of the Japanese carrier fleet was another primary objective. The IJN had been hoarding its carriers for almost 20 months, and its commitment to defend the Marianas was planned to be a decisive encounter with the USN. In only ten days in mid-June, the Americans realized all their major objectives and the IJN suffered a decisive defeat. Most of its carriers escaped, but their aircraft and trained aircrews did not. This effectively meant the end of the IJN as a major threat to future American moves in the Pacific and led directly to the desperate and ill-conceived Japanese plan to defend Leyte in October that resulted in the final destruction of the IJN.

ORIGINS OF THE CAMPAIGN

The Japanese advance during the initial period of the war was short lived. By August 1942, the Americans launched their first offensive in the Pacific, landing on Guadalcanal in the Solomon Islands. This resulted in a grinding battle of attrition that exacted heavy naval and air losses from the IJN. Losses to the USN were actually greater, but by late 1942 the flood of new American naval construction was reaching the Pacific and was already underwriting an accelerated American offensive. This increased strength could sustain offensives on two fronts. One was already underway, running up the Solomon Islands and then through New Guinea toward the Philippines and eventually China. The other was just starting from Hawaii through the Central Pacific. This basic outline for a two-front offensive against the Japanese for 1943–44 was approved at the Trident Conference held in Washington, DC on May 12–17, 1943, by the Combined Chiefs of Staff from the United States and Great Britain.

The Central Pacific axis of advance was always the preferred option for the USN. It was a predominantly naval show under the command of Admiral Chester W. Nimitz, the Commander in Chief, Pacific Ocean Areas and of the United States Pacific Fleet. Admiral Ernest J. King, Chief of Naval Operations and Commander in Chief, United States Fleet, who was a trusted advisor of President Franklin Roosevelt and a member of the Combined Chiefs of Staff, strongly supported the Central Pacific option. However, lack of resources and command rivalry in the Pacific forced an alteration of the plans for a Central Pacific offensive. The original plan coming out of the Trident Conference called for the seizure of the Marshall Islands and the Caroline Islands. By July 1943, it was obvious that an attack on the Marshalls was logistically infeasible without drawing forces from the Southwest Pacific Area command under the control of General Douglas MacArthur, so the US Joint Chiefs ordered Nimitz to attack the Gilbert Islands instead with a target date of November 15, 1943.

This modified scheme was approved at the Quebec Conference held in Canada from August 17 to 24, 1943, and future Central Pacific operations were confirmed as sequential invasions of the Gilberts, Marshalls, Carolines, and then the Palau Islands. King was successful in inserting the Marianas as a possible substitute for the Palaus. After the conference, King was supported by General Henry H. Arnold, commander of the Army Air Forces, who wanted to use the Marianas as a base for mounting B-29 bomber attacks against Japan. The new B-29 had the range to fly from the Marianas to the Japanese Home Islands. Earlier attempts to get the B-29s within range of Japan by basing them in China had demonstrated the immense logistical challenges inherent in basing heavy bombers in a place where air supply was the primary method of moving the massive amount of the required men and supplies. It was apparent that if the Army Air Forces wanted to strike Japan, establishing bases in the Marianas was the only way to do it.

By the Cairo Conference of December 1943, the Allied leaders clearly saw the advantages of the Central Pacific drive and the benefits of seizing the Marianas in particular. The attack on the Marianas was scheduled for October 1944, following the seizure of the Marshalls in January and Truk in July. A Central Pacific campaign plan was issued by Nimitz's staff in December 1943 and revised in January 1944 with a projected November 1 invasion of the Marianas.

As the pace of operations quickened, the debate between Nimitz and MacArthur became more heated. At a planning conference in Washington, DC in February and March, the schedule for Central Pacific operations was examined again and altered significantly. MacArthur's staff fought for an advance along northern New Guinea into Mindanao in the Philippines. King was determined to keep his Central Pacific drive as the primary focus. When Nimitz joined the conference, he proposed two possible schedules for the remainder of the year. One called for Truk to be bypassed, Saipan in the Marianas to be attacked by June 15, and landings on the Palaus on October 1.

What was agreed to by the Joint Chiefs of Staff was Nimitz's short-term schedule, mixed with MacArthur's longer-term goal of invading Mindanao. The final sequence of operations was set as the occupation of Hollandia on the coast of northern New Guinea by MacArthur's forces with support from Nimitz's carriers on April 15, the bypassing of Truk, followed by the initial landings on the Marianas on June 15. Following this, the next targets were the Palaus in mid-September and Mindanao in mid-November.

As the Allied command staffs pondered the next move of the rising American tide in the Pacific, the advance continued to roll forward. On November 20, 1943 Tarawa and Makin Atolls in the Gilberts were invaded and fell within days. On January 31, 1944, Nimitz's forces landed on Kwajalein Atoll in the Marshalls. Eniwetok in the western Marshalls was seized after an operation beginning on February 17. Fighting was bitter on some of these islands, particularly on Tarawa, but at no point did the IJN attempt to mount a counterattack, and the issue was never in doubt on any of the islands with the possible exception of Tarawa.

PRELIMINARY OPERATIONS

In the period leading up to the invasion of the Marianas, the Americans sought to weaken the Japanese defenses in the Central Pacific. The chief instrument for this process was the USN's Fast Carrier Task Force (also known as Task Force (TF) 58) which was growing ever stronger and demonstrating its ability to project power against Japanese shore bases with relative immunity. These efforts were successful in weakening the Japanese position in the Central Pacific and undermining their defensive scheme for holding the Marianas.

After supporting the invasion of the Marshalls from January 29 through February 6, 1944, TF 58 conducted its largest and most impressive operation of the war to date. This was the first strike on Truk in the Carolines on February 17–18, 1944. Truk was the IJN's primary anchorage from July 1942 and possessed three large airfields. Alerted by American air reconnaissance over the atoll, the IJN moved the Combined Fleet to Palau in

Japanese planes burn on a Saipan airfield on February 23, 1944 during the first American carrier raid on the Marianas. A6M Zero fighters and G4M Betty bombers can be identified. TF 58 mounted a prolonged and successful campaign to weaken Japanese land-based air power before the invasion of the Marianas in June. (Naval History and Heritage Command)

early February. When TF 58 showed up some 90nm east of Truk on the morning of February 17, there were still plenty of targets present. After seizing air control over the atoll in the morning strikes, USN attention turned to the shipping present in the lagoon. The result of 1,250 sorties over the two days was impressive – two light cruisers, four destroyers and some 30 auxiliaries and merchant ships for a total of over 200,000 tons. In return, USN aircraft losses were light and Japanese air attacks succeeded in damaging a single fleet carrier with a torpedo. The strikes by TF 58's nine carriers were the largest of the war to date and provided a portent of future attractions.

The first American attacks on the Marianas were conducted by two task groups of TF 58 on Tinian and Guam in the Marianas on February 22. The Americans claimed a large number of Japanese aircraft in the air and on the ground. The next target for TF 58 was Palau on March 30 and April 1. Again, the IJN surmised that an attack was forthcoming, so successfully moved the Combined Fleet out in time. The remaining merchant ships and auxiliaries were pummeled and 36, totaling 130,000 tons, were sunk. Japanese air losses were also heavy. In return, TF 58 suffered no damage, and USN air losses were light.

The rampage of the fast carriers continued on April 21–22 when they supported MacArthur's landing at Hollandia. By the end of the month, TF 58 had grown to 12 carriers (five fleet and seven light). If any further demonstration of its growing power was needed, TF 58 made a return strike against Truk on April 29–30 with 2,200 sorties. No large Japanese ships were present, but almost 100 Japanese aircraft were destroyed and facilities ashore flattened. After a few smaller strikes on Marcus and Wake Islands, TF 58 returned to the anchorage at Majuro for a short break before the invasion of the Marianas.

Essex turns in formation with other Task Force 58 ships, May 27, 1944, during maneuvers prior to the Marianas operation. Note her deck load of SB2C Helldivers and TBF Avengers. The ships astern are light carrier *San Jacinto* and fleet carrier *Wasp*. (Naval History and Heritage Command)

CHRONOLOGY

1944

May 20 United States lands on Biak Island off northwest New Guinea.

June 2–4 129 Japanese aircraft attack the landing force with no effect; these are the same aircraft dedicated for defense of the Marianas.

June 6 Task Force (TF) 58 departs Majuro for the Marianas.

June 7 Final planning conference between Admiral Spruance and his principal commanders before commencement of Operation *Forager* – the invasion of the Marianas.

June 11 TF 58 sends 216 aircraft to attack Japanese airfields on Saipan and Tinian.

June 12–13 TF 58 pounds airfields on Saipan, Tinian and Guam; a Japanese air attack on TF 58 on June 12 is ineffective.

June 13 Elements of TF 58 conduct a shore bombardment of Saipan.

Japanese First Mobile Fleet departs advanced base at Tawi-Tawi; spotted by American submarine.

June 15 Japanese air attacks on TF 58 from Guam and Yap Islands ineffective.

United States Marines land on Saipan and secure a beachhead.

Japanese activate Operation *A-Go* – the defense of the Marianas; First Mobile Fleet departs the Guimaras and enters Philippine Sea later that day where it is spotted by an American submarine.

June 15–16 Two task groups of TF 58 attack airfields on the Bonin Islands to cut off Japanese air reinforcement to the Marianas.

June 17 Submarine *Cavalla* sights the First Mobile Fleet 700nm west of Guam; this is the only firm locating information given to Spruance until the start of the battle.

June 18 Admiral Ozawa maneuvers the First Mobile Fleet to within 400nm of TF 58; Spruance maintains position near Saipan.

June 19 0038hrs: final decision by Spruance to fight a defensive battle and let Ozawa strike first.

0445hrs: Japanese launch first wave of search aircraft and gain contact on TF 58.

0530hrs: Japanese launch third wave of search aircraft; these later report two contacts both of which are erroneous.

0530–1000hrs: American Hellcat fighters active over Guam disrupt any attempt by Japanese land-based aircraft to attack TF 58.

0830hrs: Japanese launch first strike of 69 aircraft; only 17 eventually return.

0856hrs: Japanese launch second attack of 128 aircraft; only 31 eventually return.

0909hrs: Japanese carrier *Taiho* hit by torpedo from submarine *Albacore*.

1000hrs: Japanese launch third attack of 47 aircraft; 40 eventually return.

1023hrs: TF 58 launches all available fighters to intercept expected waves of Japanese aircraft.

1035hrs: first Japanese attack intercepted and some 25 are shot down.

1049hrs: surviving Japanese aircraft attack Task Group (TG) 58.7 and score one hit on battleship *South Dakota* and near misses on two cruisers.

1100hrs: Japanese launch fourth attack of 82 aircraft.

1107hrs: Japanese second attack detected on radar.

1139hrs: Hellcats intercept second raid and down some 70 aircraft.

Around 1200hrs: remnants of second raid attack TG 58.2, TG 58.3 and TG 58.7 and inflict only minor damage on carriers *Wasp* and *Bunker Hill*.

1222hrs: submarine *Cavalla* torpedoes carrier *Shokaku*.

1255hrs: Hellcats intercept third Japanese attack that is conducting a search for targets north of TF 58.

1423hrs: Japanese fourth raid fails to find the reported contact south of TF 58; a small group stumbles on TG 58.2 en route to an airfield in the Marianas and launches an ineffective attack.

1449hrs: 49 aircraft from the Japanese fourth attack arrive over Guam and are attacked by Hellcats; 30 are shot down and the other 19 are wrecked upon landing.

1501hrs: *Shokaku* sinks with heavy loss of life.

1532hrs: massive explosion on *Taiho*; the carrier later sinks.

2000hrs: TF 58 heads west to engage First Mobile Force.

June 20

June 21

June 22

0530hrs: TF 58 launches morning search but fails to find First Mobile Fleet.

0920hrs: Japanese attempt to begin refueling in preparation for further attacks on TF 58 the following day.

1200hrs: special long-range search by TF 58 unsuccessful.

1330hrs: TF 58 launches afternoon search.

1540hrs: First Mobile Fleet spotted by TF 58 aircraft; Spruance agrees to launch all-out attack.

1624hrs: TF 58 launches 216 aircraft to attack First Mobile Fleet.

1645hrs: Ozawa orders high speed to the northwest to avoid attack.

1715hrs: Japanese search aircraft spot TF 58; ten torpedo aircraft ordered to make a dusk attack.

1840-1910: TF 58 strike spots the First Mobile Fleet and makes a series of hasty attacks; carrier *Hiyo* hit by a torpedo, two other carriers and two escorts damaged, and two oilers hit and later scuttled.

2032hrs: *Hiyo* sinks.

2045hrs: TF 58 begins recovery of its strike which takes two hours; 80 aircraft are lost to operational cases in addition to 20 lost in combat.

2046hrs: Ozawa ordered to break off action.

2030hrs: Spruance orders TF 58 to abandon chase.

First Mobile Fleet arrives at Okinawa.

OPPOSING COMMANDERS

UNITED STATES NAVY

The battle of the Philippine Sea was fought under the strategic direction of **Admiral Chester Nimitz** in his capacity as the Commander in Chief, Pacific Ocean Areas and of the United States Pacific Fleet. Pacific Ocean Areas was divided into three commands, Northern, Central and Southern. The Central area included the Marianas. Nimitz retained this command until mid-1943 when responsibility was given to Admiral Raymond A. Spruance.

In his capacity as Commander in Chief, United States Pacific Fleet, Nimitz retained control of all naval forces in the Pacific. The Fifth Fleet was created in April 1944 and Spruance was placed in command. The subordinate parts of the Fifth Fleet were Joint Expeditionary Forces (TF 51) under Vice Admiral R. K. Turner, Forward Area, Central Pacific (TF 57) under Vice Admiral John

From left to right: Admiral Raymond A. Spruance, Vice Admiral Marc A. Mitscher, Fleet Admiral Chester W. Nimitz, and Vice Admiral Willis A. Lee on Spruance's flagship *Indianapolis* in February 1945. Nimitz set the objectives for Spruance and his Fifth Fleet to achieve, while Mitscher was in tactical command of the Fast Carrier Task Force. Lee was the USN's premier gunnery expert and assumed command of TF 58's battle line when it was formed. (Naval History and Heritage Command)

H. Hoover, and most importantly Fast Carrier Forces (TF 58) under Vice Admiral Marc A. Mitscher. Submarine forces were subordinate to Submarine Force, Pacific Fleet (TF 17) under Vice Admiral Charles A. Lockwood.

The American command team was a highly effective instrument by mid-1944. The principal reason for this was Nimitz who was without doubt one of the most outstanding, if not the most outstanding, leaders in USN history.

Nimitz took command of the Pacific Fleet on December 31, 1941 and immediately set about the task of turning around American naval fortunes in the Pacific following Pearl Harbor. Not usually known for his aggressiveness, he was in fact very aggressive as evident at Coral Sea and Midway when he committed his precious carriers against larger Japanese forces. The famous USN victory at Midway was his design. He was known as a calm leader who worked well with subordinates and considered their views. Nimitz was not a meddler and had a gift for choosing the right people and then letting them get on with their jobs.

The most important USN command figure in the battle was **Admiral Raymond A. Spruance** who commanded the Fifth Fleet. Spruance gained flag rank in 1940 and was known in the pre-war Navy as a thinker and strategist. Filling in for Vice Admiral William F. Halsey at the battle of Midway, he was given credit for the victory. After the battle, Spruance was appointed as Nimitz's chief of staff before being assigned to command the Central Pacific Force in August 1943, which later became the Fifth Fleet in April 1944. He possessed many traits of a great commander. He was known as an intellectual with a sharp mind who was able to coolly think through all courses of action before making a decision. He gave his staff great decision-making powers since he approached problems from a larger perspective. He shunned the limelight and by design was remote from his staff, and especially the press. If any shortcoming could be found in Spruance, it was an abundance of caution. This had served him well during the final stages of the battle of Midway, but would turn out not to be a virtue in June 1944.

Vice Admiral Marc Mitscher was the commander of Task Force 58, the USN's fast carrier force. He was much like Spruance in that he was unassuming and did not seek personal glory. He possessed the ability to inspire and lead men. Mitscher was one of the pioneers of US naval aviation and had considerable experience as a carrier commander and a carrier task force commander. He had commanded the carrier *Hornet* at Midway, and then commanded land-based air forces in the Solomons. Returning to sea, he led TF 58 through the Marshalls and Truk operations when the USN learned how to conduct strike operations against large Japanese land-based air forces. By mid-1944, he was

Vice Admiral Marc A. Mitscher was the very capable commander of Task Force 58 during the battle. This picture was taken after the battle in February 1945 and shows Mitscher, right, with his chief of staff Commodore Arleigh A. Burke aboard carrier *Bunker Hill*. The two formed a good command team at Philippine Sea and were responsible for the operations of the USN's most powerful fighting unit. (Naval History and Heritage Command)

Rear Admiral Joseph J. "Jocko" Clark (center) led TG 58.1 during the battle. He conducted the pre-battle raid on the Bonin Islands to cut the flow of Japanese air reinforcements to the battle area and was considered the most capable and aggressive of Mitscher's task group commanders. (Naval History and Heritage Command)

at the peak of his game but suffered occasionally from a high degree of oversight from Spruance, which reduced Mitscher's role. If Mitscher had a flaw, it was that he was not always attentive to details.

Mitscher's carrier task group commanders were **Rear Admiral James "Jocko" Clark** (TG 58.1), **Rear Admiral Alfred E. Montgomery** (TG 58.2), **Rear Admiral John W. Reeves** (TG 58.3) and **Rear Admiral William K. Harrill** (TG 58.4). Clark was especially aggressive, was recognized as a skilled carrier commander, and went on to command carriers through the Korean War. Montgomery served until the end of 1944 on carrier duty.

Vice Admiral Charles A. Lockwood (center) was Commander Submarine Force, Pacific Fleet during the battle. He is shown welcoming submarine *Balao* back from a war cruise, probably at Guam in early 1945. Lockwood's submarines had a dramatic impact on the battle, both providing critical reconnaissance data and attacking Ozawa's fleet. (Naval History and Heritage Command)

Reeves was rotated out of his command after the battle. Harrill failed to perform aggressively during the battle and handled his task group poorly. He fell ill on June 29 and returned to the United States never to return to a carrier command. The battle line was commanded by **Vice Admiral W. A. Lee** who was considered the USN's leading gunnery expert and who had used this skill to defeat a Japanese surface force with two modern USN battleships in a key battle in the Guadalcanal campaign.

Another important USN command figure was **Vice Admiral Charles A. Lockwood** who was Commander, Submarine Force, Pacific Fleet from February 1943. He was an aggressive commander who inspired devotion from his submarine crews and was largely responsible for overcoming technical and personnel issues to make American submarines arguably the most effective force in the Pacific. Lockwood's submarines assigned to support the invasion of the Marianas played an important part in the battle.

IMPERIAL JAPANESE NAVY

The organization responsible for operational control of the Japanese armed forces was the Imperial General Headquarters. This included sections from the Imperial Japanese Army and Imperial Japanese Navy. Despite the fears of the IJN that the Imperial General Headquarters would usurp its operational independence, this was not the case and the IJN retained a high degree of autonomy. The Imperial General Headquarters was unsuccessful in reconciling the different views of the Imperial Japanese Army (IJA)and IJN, but it did foster some degree of cooperation. This cooperation was most effective at the highest level since any decision reached by the Imperial General Headquarters had to be unanimous. At lower levels, cooperation between the IJA and IJN was usually poor.

The Naval General Staff, which also doubled as the navy section of the Imperial General Headquarters, was responsible for strategic and operational planning for the IJN. This body issued orders to the Combined Fleet, which was the IJN's offensive force. **Admiral Toyoda Soemu** who took command in May 1944 led the Combined Fleet in this battle.

Toyoda was seen by other IJN officers as both uncompromising and difficult to work with. Nevertheless, he was also highly regarded as a man of considerable experience and capability who had steadily risen through the ranks. He gained flag rank in 1931, by 1941

The Commander in Chief of the Combined Fleet was Admiral Toyoda Soemu shown here aboard his flagship light cruiser *Oyodo* about September 1944. He was responsible for producing the plans for *A-Go* and the even more unrealistic and disastrous plan to defend the Philippines only a few months later. (Naval History and Heritage Command)

was a full admiral and seemed poised to get the job as commander of the Combined Fleet. After Admiral Yamamoto Isoroku was appointed to this post, Toyoda spent the first parts of the war in shore commands, but after the death of Combined Fleet Commander Admiral Koga Mineichi in March 1944, the IJN turned to Toyoda. He assumed command of the Combined Fleet on May 3, 1944 and held this post until the following May when he became Chief of the Naval General Staff. He thoughtfully sought a way to turn around the IJN's fortunes but was not an effective strategist and presided over the disaster at the Philippine Sea and the crushing defeat at Leyte Gulf in October 1944.

The most important IJN command figure in the battle was **Vice Admiral Ozawa Jisaburo** who commanded the First Mobile Fleet. He was also in direct tactical command of Carrier Division 1 and oversaw all IJN carriers – a great deal to do for a single officer. Ozawa remains largely unknown but he was one of the IJN's most capable officers of the entire war. His original career path was as a torpedo specialist but, by the start of the war, he was an aviation advocate. Following a tour as the Combined Fleet's chief of staff, he assumed command of Carrier Division 1 in 1940. At the start of the war, he was given one of the IJN's most important naval tasks, to secure Malaya and the Dutch East Indies as commander of the Southern Expeditionary Fleet. He was successful in this mission, and then conducted a devastating raid into the Bay of Bengal in April 1942. He resumed his focus on aviation when he was appointed as commander of the Third Fleet (the force with most of the IJN's carriers) in November 1942 that led to his command of the First Mobile Fleet in mid-1944. After his defeat at Philippine Sea, he offered to resign, but this offer was refused and by war's end he had assumed command of the Combined Fleet.

ABOVE LEFT
Vice Admiral Ozawa Jisaburo was responsible for executing *A-Go*. Despite handling his forces as well as could be expected, he experienced a shattering defeat. (Naval History and Heritage Command)

ABOVE RIGHT
Vice Admiral Kurita Takeo commanded the Van Force (Force C) which was the largest component of the First Mobile Fleet during the battle. Had his advice to Ozawa been heeded for an early retreat on June 20, the American strike later in the day could not have occurred. (Naval History and Heritage Command)

Ozawa's task force commanders were all veterans of previous Pacific War battles. **Vice Admiral Kurita Takeo** commanded the Van Force, which comprised the bulk of thc First Mobile Fleet's battleships. Kurita was a surface warfare officer who had commanded a squadron of heavy cruisers at the start of the war. This squadron participated in the invasion of the Dutch East Indies and Midway where his cruisers were pummeled by USN carrier aircraft. He was in command of a division of battleships from July 1942 to July 1943, and conducted a successful bombardment of Henderson Field on Guadalcanal and carried out carrier screening duties. Kurita assumed command of the Second Fleet in August 1943 and this led to his appointment as Van Force commander. In October 1944 at the battle of Leyte Gulf, he was in command of the First Diversionary Attack Force that included the bulk of the IJN's heavy ships. He declined to make a suicidal and largely ceremonial attack into Leyte Gulf after an unsuccessful action off Samar against USN escort carriers.

Part of the Van Force was Carrier Division 3 commanded by **Rear Admiral Obayashi Sueo.** He was a long-time aviation advocate who had held a succession of aviation billets since 1936 including command of light carrier *Zuiho* at Midway and Santa Cruz. Promoted to rear admiral in May 1943, he assumed command of Carrier Division 3 in February 1944. He was known as particularly aggressive and later became one of the driving forces behind the IJN's adoption of kamikaze tactics. **Rear Admiral Joshima Takaji**, commander of Carrier Division 2, began the war as captain of carrier *Shokaku* and fought at Coral Sea. He went on to command a seaplane tender division during the Guadalcanal campaign before assuming command of Carrier Division 2 in September 1943.

The Sixth Fleet, the IJN's submarine force that was headquartered on Saipan, was commanded by **Vice Admiral Takagi Takeo.** Before the battle, Takagi successfully executed key aspects of the Japanese invasion of the Dutch East Indies including command at the battle of Java Sea. He commanded the Carrier Striking Force at Coral Sea and was present at Midway. He returned to an operational command on June 21, 1943 with his appointment to command the Sixth Fleet. He was caught on Saipan by the American invasion and killed.

The local defense forces in the Marianas were subordinate to the Central Pacific Area Fleet under **Vice Admiral Nagumo Chuichi.** This same admiral had commanded the IJN's carrier force at three of the previous four carrier battles of the war: Midway, Eastern Solomons and Santa Cruz. He did not have any aviation experience before the war, but by October 1942 following Santa Cruz he was the most experienced commander of large carrier forces of any admiral, Japanese or American. His mixed record of success and failure led to his relief in November 1942 after which he was relegated to the backwater assignment on the Marianas. He was trapped on Saipan and committed suicide when the island fell to the Americans.

The commander of the IJN's land-based air forces during the battle, the First Air Fleet, was **Rear Admiral Kakuta Kakuji.** He was familiar with naval aviation having served as a carrier division commander at Midway and Guadalcanal. He assumed command of the First Air Fleet in July 1943 and at the start of the battle had his headquarters on Tinian. He played an important part in the battle by continually misleading Ozawa on the success and status of the land-based air forces in the Marianas. Kakuta was later killed on August 2, 1944 in the final stages of the battle for Tinian.

OPPOSING FLEETS

The battle of the Philippine Sea was the result of the IJN's latest attempt to force a decisive battle with the US Pacific Fleet. However, by June 1944, the IJN faced a severe numerical disadvantage as shown in this table.

Strength Comparison, June 19, 1944

	First Mobile Force	Task Force 58
Airpower		
Fleet carriers	5	7
Light carriers	4	8
Fighters/fighter-bombers	206	475
Dive-bombers	109	232
Torpedo bombers	78	184
Reconnaissance aircraft	14	
Total carrier aircraft	407	891
Surface combatants		
Battleships	5	7
Heavy cruisers	11	8
Light cruisers	3	13
Destroyers	27	56
Total combatants	46	84

Essex was the lead ship of the largest class of fleet carriers ever built. Fourteen of these ships saw action during the Pacific War. This photo is from August 30, 1943 as the carrier was en route to a raid on Marcus Island. A recovery is underway – note the Avenger aft of the island. The key to carrying a large air group was using a deck park since not all of the 90–100 aircraft onboard could be accommodated in the hangar deck. (Naval History and Heritage Command)

This table does not even take into account the qualitative superiority enjoyed by the USN in almost all warfare areas which will be discussed below. Likewise, it also does not include the USN forces assigned to provide direct support to the landings. Before the carrier battle, Spruance dispatched five heavy cruisers, three light cruisers and 13 destroyers to reinforce TF 58's screen. This left seven old battleships, one heavy cruiser, two light cruisers, and 13 destroyers to protect the landing area. These were supported by eight escort carriers (escorted by 12 destroyers) which operated some 170 aircraft. Another three escort carriers and four destroyers were held in reserve.

Yorktown underway during the Marianas operation in June 1944. The ship is painted in a Measure 33, Design 10a camouflage scheme. Note the large number of antiaircraft guns positioned along the flight deck and fore and aft of the island. (Naval History and Heritage Command)

THE US NAVY

Organization

In June 1944, TF 58 was the most powerful naval force on the planet. It was broken down into four subordinate task groups, each with one or two fleet carriers and two light carriers. In direct support was an escort of three or four light or heavy cruisers, and eight to 13 destroyers. When the prospect of an encounter with the IJN appeared likely, TF 58 formed a battle line. This was a separate task force formed from the screens of the four carrier task groups and included seven modern battleships (all commissioned after 1941), four heavy cruisers and 13 destroyers.

Enterprise underway on November 24, 1943 while supporting the invasion of the Gilbert Islands. Of the USN's seven pre-war carriers, she was the only one operating with TF 58 at Philippine Sea. Though unable to carry as many aircraft as Essex-class carriers, she remained a powerful unit and operated with the Fast Carrier Task Force for the remainder of the war. (Naval History and Heritage Command)

Light carrier *Belleau Wood* underway in December 1943. The ship was a member of the nine-ship Independence class, which were conversions from Cleveland-class light cruisers. These ships proved very successful in service providing an insurance policy until the bulk of the Essex class entered service. Eight of these ships fought at Philippine Sea. (Naval History and Heritage Command)

Carriers

Six of TF 58's fleet carriers were newly commissioned Essex-class ships. These were introduced into combat in August 1943; they transformed the fighting in the Pacific and spearheaded the American advance for the remainder of the war. Essex-class carriers were the most powerful ships of the war, and certainly the best carrier design of the era. They possessed a good balance of striking power, speed and endurance, as well as defensive capabilities. The key attribute of these ships was their large air group of over 90 aircraft. This massive offensive punch was combined with a top speed of 33 knots, a range of over 15,000nm and a heavy antiaircraft protection of 12 5in./38 guns and as many as 72 40mm and 58 20mm guns. Task Force 58's final fleet carrier was the veteran pre-war construction *Enterprise* which possessed capabilities broadly similar to the Essex class.

The Independence-class carriers displaced 15,100 tons full load, carried a typical air group of 33 aircraft, were armed with 26 40mm and 40 20mm guns and could steam at a top speed of 33 knots. This is *Princeton*; the carrier was sunk at Leyte Gulf in October making her the only USN fleet or light carrier lost after 1942. (Naval History and Heritage Command)

Augmenting the fleet carriers were the Independence-class light carriers, eight of which were available for the battle. These ships were the result of a crash conversion program based on the hulls of Cleveland-class light cruisers. The result was a very useful conversion that provided a carrier able to embark an air wing of 34 aircraft on a fast, well-protected hull. These light carriers proved successful in service and were superior to comparable IJN light carrier conversions.

Carrier air groups and aircraft

The large, over 90-aircraft air group of the Essex class was broken down into three squadrons. In mid-1944, these consisted of a 36-aircraft fighter squadron, a 36-aircraft dive-bomber squadron and a torpedo-bomber squadron of another 18 aircraft. Often these squadrons went into combat over strength. There was also a detachment of four radar-equipped night fighters. Each light carrier embarked a smaller air group of 25 fighters and nine torpedo planes. In practice, the light carrier air groups were often used to provide combat air patrol over the task force to free up the larger fleet carrier air groups for strike missions.

The typical search range of USN carrier aircraft was about 325nm. This was attained by carrying extra fuel instead of ordnance. The only real weakness in USN carrier air wings was their short strike range. Depending on a number of tactical conditions, this was between 150 and 200nm.

The standard 1944 USN carrier fighter was the Grumman F6F-3 Hellcat. The Hellcat entered combat service in late 1943 and was far superior to the IJN's Mitsubishi A6M2 "Zero" fighter. The American fighter was more rugged and able to take considerable punishment, carried a heavy armament of six .50-cal. machine guns, and used the powerful Pratt & Whitney R-2800 engine which allowed it to gain dominance over the once-vaunted Zero. The Zero remained a superior dogfighter, but the Hellcat's superior speed and firepower made it unbeatable if used properly.

The USN's most potent carrier strike aircraft for the early-war period was the Douglas SBD Dauntless dive-bomber. The aircraft was supremely reliable, easy to fly, could carry a large payload, and was a steady dive-bombing platform. By the middle of 1944, the latest version of the Dauntless, the SBD-5, remained in only two squadrons. Replacing the much-loved Dauntless was the Curtiss SB2C Helldiver. The Helldiver was a much larger aircraft than the Dauntless that promised a heavier payload and greater speed. Early

flight-testing in 1941 revealed many problems, and an excessively long gestation period ensued. Not until the SB2C-3 version with its larger engine and other modifications was the aircraft truly combat ready.

The Grumman TBF/TBM Avenger was the best carrier torpedo aircraft of the war. Work on this design had begun before the war, and after Midway it became the standard USN carrier torpedo plane. It proved reliable in service, able to withstand battle damage, and by mid-1944 it carried a reliable torpedo. It was also versatile and was able to perform as a torpedo plane or a conventional bomber.

Training

The average level of training for a USN carrier pilot was quite high in 1944, and certainly far superior to that of the IJN. US Navy pilots had two years of cockpit time and 350 hours of air time before they were even sent to a carrier air group. Further increasing the effectiveness of this training was the USN practice of pulling back experienced pilots from the front lines and placing them in training billets where they could pass on their experience to new aircrews. Once a pilot joined a carrier air group, up to another year could be spent training the air group to work together before it embarked on a carrier and was sent to war. By June 1944, almost all USN pilots in TF 58 were combat veterans. This experience was gained in high-tempo operations in the months before the battle.

Antiaircraft defenses

US Navy antiaircraft defenses had made significant advances since the beginning of the war. In the first four carrier battles, these defenses had generally proved unable to defend the fleet's few and precious carriers. On each occasion, IJN strike aircraft were able to penetrate USN combat air patrol (CAP) and antiaircraft fire to deliver punishing, and occasionally fatal, blows against American carriers.

The most effective method of defeating Japanese air attack was placing CAP in advance of the incoming strike. For various reasons the art of fighter direction is difficult, and early American efforts in this area were haphazard. Among the problems were inadequate radar warning, incorrect altitude placement of fighter aircraft, and faulty communications procedures which made it difficult or impossible to give orders to airborne aircraft. During 1942, USN fighter direction improved by trial and error, and by mid-1944 a

ABOVE LEFT
A Helldiver SB2C-3 variant pictured in 1945 from *Hancock*. After a long gestation period, the Helldiver proved to be reliable and tough in service. Some 175 were present at Philippine Sea. (Naval History and Heritage Command)

ABOVE RIGHT
The USN's standard torpedo bomber in June 1944 was the TBF/TBM Avenger and some 190 were present at Philippine Sea. It was very successful, being the most produced naval strike aircraft in history. The aircraft possessed a top speed of 267mph and the capability to carry 2,000 pounds of bombs or torpedoes. In this view, an Avenger of VT-51 from *San Jacinto* takes off on June 28 to raid Guam. (Naval History and Heritage Command)

An attacking Japanese aircraft goes down in flames between two American carriers on June 19. Of the approximately 20 aircraft that broke through the CAP to attack an American carrier, none could score a direct hit. (Naval History and Heritage Command)

solid doctrine was in place to maximize the chances of gaining an interception with CAP. During the battle, TF 58 ran a centralized fighter-direction scheme under the control of the fighter-direction officer on Mitscher's flagship *Lexington*. Working with the fighter-direction officers in the other task groups and on each carrier it was possible to shift available fighters from the control of one task group to the other while still keeping a central reserve to handle future raids. At the time of the battle, TF 58 was in the process of upgrading to new VHF radio equipment that meant that only two fighter-direction channels were common to all four carrier groups. Despite this potential limitation, fighter direction was handled to a high standard with most Japanese raids met by fighters as far as 60 miles from the carriers with the defending Hellcats deployed to give them an altitude advantage.

The standard air-warning radar installed on carriers and battleships was the SK radar that could regularly detect formations of enemy aircraft flying at higher altitudes out to 100nm and frequently beyond. The SM radar fitted aboard carriers could provide indications of height. Radar performance was often uneven and subject to environmental conditions, but was most effective against Japanese aircraft flying at higher altitudes over water away from land features, like the conditions that would prevail at Philippine Sea. During the battle, USN air-warning radar performed well. The Japanese deployed "window" (the original name for chaff which is a radar countermeasures tactic that uses thin pieces of aluminum) to present a radar operator with many false returns during the battle to confuse American radar operators, but this had only a minor effect.

Those Japanese aircraft surviving CAP interception were then subject to antiaircraft fire as they made their attack runs. US Navy task groups used a circular formation in the face of air attack with the carriers deployed in the center of the formation. This formation allowed for defense in depth and all-around protection, and also enabled the entire task group to change direction easily. The outer edge of antiaircraft protection was provided by the 5in./38 gun which was radar-controlled by the Mark 37 Director and effective out to 10,000 yards. The 40mm gun fitted in either dual or quad mounts provided intermediate protection. This weapon was director-controlled and effective out to 3,000 yards. Final protection was the job of the 20mm gun fitted in single mounts in large numbers on all USN combatants. When fitted with the Mark 14 gyro-sight, the 20mm was much more effective. The weapon was limited to an effective range of less than 1,500 yards.

US Navy antiaircraft weaponry was very effective in deterring or defeating Japanese air attacks. Even in 1942, the introduction of the 40mm gun, additional 20mm mounts and additional fire-control radars resulted in heavy attrition to Japanese strike aircraft. The net effect was to make Japanese air attack on the Fast Carrier Task Force ineffective and extremely costly. From November 1943 until June 1944, 195 IJN aircraft made daylight attacks on the carriers and 40 percent were destroyed. In return, 5 percent of Japanese aircraft hit their targets. At Philippine Sea, 60 IJN aircraft made attacks on American warships, and only five scored hits or damaging near misses.

Surface combatants

While the main striking power of TF 58 came from its carriers, Spruance and Mitscher also saw a major role for the task force's surface combatants. Doctrinally, the battleships were formed into a separate task group and deployed in advance of the carrier groups. This could act as a lure for Japanese aircraft heading for the carriers, but most importantly it placed the battleships in the van where they were best positioned to engage IJN surface forces. The battle line could also finish off any cripples created by USN carrier strikes.

Battleship *Washington* was Vice Admiral Lee's flagship for the battle. Both her and her sister ship, *North Carolina* were present for Operation *Forager*. *Washington* had the distinction of being the only USN modern battleship to engage a Japanese battleship during the war when she sank *Kirishima* off Guadalcanal in November 1942. This April 1944 view provides a good look at her 16in. main battery and 5in. secondary battery. (Naval History and Heritage Command)

The battle line comprised seven battleships, all modern since they were all commissioned after 1941. These carried 16in. naval guns and the best fire-control systems in existence. They were also extremely well protected against both air and surface attack. US Navy heavy cruisers came in two varieties – the Treaty cruisers built before the war and the wartime construction of the Baltimore class. Treaty cruisers were inferior to their IJN counterparts, primarily because of a lack of protection, but did possess a useful antiaircraft suite. The Baltimore-class heavy cruisers, of which three were assigned to TF 58, were the best heavy cruisers of the war with a fine mix of protection, antisurface and antiair capabilities. USN light cruisers assigned to TF 58 were all modern. The four Atlanta-class ships were used in primarily an antiaircraft role, and the nine 10,000-ton Cleveland class carried the 6in. gun with a high rate of fire and possessed superior antiaircraft capabilities. They were clearly superior to any IJN light cruiser. American destroyers were also largely wartime construction and carried a significant antiaircraft battery. After an uncertain start with their torpedoes, these problems had been fixed and a new doctrine employed to use them in conjunction with radar. All factors considered, the USN carried a significant edge in surface firepower into the battle. This would have been especially apparent in a day engagement, but the widespread use of radar would have also given the

Indiana seen in January 1944 from a SB2C Helldiver. Three of the four South Dakota-class battleships were assigned to TF 58 for Operation *Forager*. These were powerful 35,000-ton ships with a main battery of nine 16in. guns and a capable antiaircraft fit of 20 5in./38 dual-purpose guns and 48 40mm guns. (Naval History and Heritage Command)

Americans an edge at night. The extent of the USN's night-fighting superiority was demonstrated a few months later at the battle of Leyte Gulf. However, the IJN's early-war advantage in night fighting and the capabilities of its destroyers at night with their heavy torpedo batteries meant that American commanders were still loath to risk a night engagement in mid-1944.

Submarines

Another significant advantage enjoyed by the USN was in the area of submarines. American submarines were crippled early in the war by deficient torpedoes, but by 1944 these problems had been rectified. The primary USN fleet submarines were those of the Gato and the Balao classes. Once equipped with torpedoes that worked, these boats could use their long range and superior radar to wreak havoc on Japanese shipping and warships. Imperial Japanese Navy antisubmarine warfare tactics and weaponry proved inadequate when it came to handling USN submarine attacks. By 1944, American submarines were commanded by a corps of aggressive skippers who had learned to pursue and attack Japanese convoys and even task forces relentlessly and with a high degree of immunity. American submarines performed their scouting and attack roles during the battle to a very high standard. TF 17 employed 18 submarines and the Seventh Fleet deployed nine more in the combat area.

Logistical support

Underpinning Operation *Forager* was a significant logistical effort. Fleet anchorages were built at Eniwetok, Kwajalein and Majuro Atolls and at Seadler Harbor in the Admiralties. On May 4, the fleet anchorage at Majuro was established. It had a large and deep anchorage, but no shore facilities. It was from here that TF 58 departed to give battle with the IJN.

Service Squadron Ten performed mobile support to the invasion force. It was charged to provide adequate provisions, ammunition and fuel to the invasion force of over 600 ships. For TF 58, arrangements were made to refuel every few days and to provide ammunition and replacement aircraft when needed. The USN organized 24 oilers, escorted by eight destroyers and 12 destroyer escorts, into eight fueling-at-sea groups. For the first time, two escort carriers were devoted to bringing replacement aircraft to TF 58. This awesome feat of logistics allowed the USN to project power over a sustained period and ensured that TF 58 would not be handicapped during the battle.

ABOVE LEFT
Light cruiser *San Juan* pictured in January 1944. At 8,340 tons full load and armed with 16 5in./38 dual-purpose guns, these ships were ideally suited to provide antiaircraft support to the carriers of TF 58. Four of these ships were present at Philippine Sea. (Naval History and Heritage Command)

ABOVE RIGHT
Nine Cleveland-class light cruisers were present at Philippine Sea, serving in the screens of all but one of TF 58 task groups. This is *Santa Fe* in December 1944. These 14,131 full load-displacement ships were powerfully armed with 12 6in. and 12 5in./38 guns. Though overcrowded and top heavy, they were the most numerous and best light cruisers of the war. (Naval History and Heritage Command)

THE IMPERIAL JAPANESE NAVY

Those parts of the Combined Fleet involved in the battle were the First Mobile Fleet, the Central Pacific Area Fleet and the land-based aircraft of the Base Air Force. The First Mobile Fleet was created on March 1, 1944. It consisted of the former First and Second Fleets, which controlled the bulk of the IJN's battleships and heavy cruisers, and the Third Fleet, which controlled the IJN's carriers. On March 10, 1944, the Central Pacific Area Fleet was established to control local defense forces and land-based air forces in the Carolines and Marianas. The First Air Fleet comprised land-based air units. This was a large force which after May 5, 1944 controlled four air flotillas (the 22nd, 23rd, 26th and 61st).

Also assigned to the operation were submarines of the 6th Fleet. These were directly subordinate to the Combined Fleet. The headquarters and maintenance of the submarine fleet had been moved from Truk to Kure in Japan earlier in 1944. Imperial Japanese Navy submarines were generally larger than their USN counterparts and designed to have great endurance to operate directly with the battle fleet. Some even had embarked aircraft for reconnaissance. These submarines were equipped with reliable torpedoes, but were generally slow to dive, carried no radar or weak radar, and were handicapped by an inappropriate doctrine: they were not deployed properly to intervene in the battle, and were massacred by USN antisubmarine forces.

Superbattleships *Yamato* and *Musashi* at anchor in Truk lagoon in 1943. These ships were designed for a decisive battle with USN battleships that never occurred. By June 1944, IJN had finally incorporated its battleships in direct support of their carriers, something the USN had done almost two years earlier. (Yamato Museum)

The First Mobile Fleet

Following the evacuation of Truk in early 1944, the bulk of the Combined Fleet was based in Singapore and the nearby Lingga Roads anchorage. Brunei Bay, in the northwest coast of British Borneo, was used as a forward staging base. The IJN later used a new fleet anchorage at Tawi-Tawi in the Sulu Archipelago in the southwest part of the Philippines. This location was better for operations in support of the Marianas.

Carrier forces

The Japanese gathered nine carriers for the upcoming battle and these were divided into three divisions. Carrier Division 1 was the centerpiece of the First Mobile Fleet with fleet carriers *Taiho*, *Shokaku* and *Zuikaku*. Carrier Division 2 was assigned the converted carriers *Junyo*, *Hiyo* and *Ryuho*. Three smaller converted carriers, *Chitose*, *Chiyoda* and *Zuiho*, comprised Carrier Division 3. Despite the availability of this unprecedented number of carriers, IJN planners estimated that their carrier force would only be marginally ready for the upcoming battle. By the end of March 1944, Carrier Division 1 would be fully capable of daytime operations with a planned 81 fighters, 81 dive-bombers, 54 attack aircraft (the Japanese terminology for torpedo aircraft) and nine reconnaissance aircraft from

the 601st Air Group. Only half of the reconnaissance aircraft would be able to conduct nighttime operations and only half the aircraft could even conduct strike operations. Carrier Division 2 embarked the even more poorly trained 652nd Air Group with a planned 81 fighters, 36 dive-bombers and 18 attack aircraft. Carrier Division 3's 653rd Air Group could operate its 63 fighters from land bases, but its attack aircraft (27 aircraft) were ill-trained to conduct strike missions from carriers. Between March and the beginning of the battle in mid-June, training opportunities were limited for IJN aviators, but the overall state of the First Mobile Fleet's air groups did improve, though not significantly.

The carriers of the First Mobile Fleet were also a mixed bag. Of the nine carriers available, only three were originally built as such. These were the three fleet carriers of Carrier Division 1 that included the two Shokaku-class

Zuikaku was commissioned in time for the Pearl Harbor attack and fought successfully at the carrier battles of Coral Sea, Eastern Solomons and Santa Cruz. She survived the battle of the Philippine Sea and was Ozawa's flagship at the battle of Leyte Gulf where four of the IJN's remaining carriers were sacrificed in an elaborate deception operation. (Yamato Museum)

ships and the new carrier *Taiho*, Ozawa's flagship. When *Shokaku* and *Zuikaku* entered service in late 1941, they were the finest carriers in the world. They could carry a large air group of over 72 aircraft, had a top speed of 34 knots, and were well protected. They participated in the Pearl Harbor attack and, after the sinking of the IJN's other four fleet carriers at Midway, were the centerpiece of the IJN's carrier force for the remainder of 1942 and 1943. *Taiho* was designed with an important improvement – an armored flight deck designed to withstand 1,000-pound bombs. The ship was still able to carry a large air group of 75 aircraft. This excellent combination of protection and striking power made her a potentially formidable adversary. Commissioned in March 1944, much was expected of her; the upcoming battle would be her first.

The two remaining large carriers of the Hiyo class (*Hiyo* and *Junyo*) were conversions from large passenger liners. As such, their speed and protection were not up to fleet carrier standards. However, they could carry a large air group of over 50 aircraft so presented a much-needed augmentation to the IJN's carrier fleet. The remaining carriers were also conversions. *Zuiho* was converted in 1940 from a submarine tender. She carried only 30 aircraft and was unprotected, but her high speed and good endurance made her useful in service. *Ryuho* was a conversion from a submarine tender completed in November 1942. Her small flight deck, low maximum speed of 26 knots, lack of protection, and small air group of some 30 aircraft made her a second-line unit. Philippine Sea was her only combat operation of the war. *Chitose* and *Chiyoda* were converted from seaplane carriers and entered the fleet as light carriers in early 1944. They possessed capabilities similar to that of *Zuiho* and carried some 30 aircraft.

Hiyo seen with sister ship *Junyo* on May 13, 1944. These ships were converted from large passenger liners and displaced 27,500 tons full load. This meant they were largely unprotected except for the addition of minimal armor around the machinery and magazine spaces and possessed a borderline top speed of 25.5 knots. Nevertheless, they were very useful additions to the IJN's carrier force since they could carry over 50 aircraft. (Yamato Museum)

Junyo fought from the Aleutians campaign in June 1942 until the end of the war. This is a view of the carrier in 1945 after the war. Her mercantile lines can be seen in this view. (Naval History and Heritage Command)

29

Ryuho was converted from a submarine tender in November 1942. She was not considered a successful carrier because of her low speed and deck characteristics. Her only combat operation was Operation A-Go; she operated primarily as an aircraft ferry. Ryuho survived the war in a damaged condition and is seen here in October 1945. (Naval History and Heritage Command)

Air groups and aircraft

Imperial Japanese Navy fleet carriers embarked an air group comprising three squadrons. These included a 27-aircraft fighter squadron, a dive-bomber squadron of 24 aircraft and a torpedo squadron with 18 aircraft. Several reconnaissance aircraft rounded out the air group. The two Hiyo-class carriers could not embark a full air group so only carried a fighter squadron with 27 aircraft, 18 dive-bombers and six torpedo aircraft. Light carriers carried 21 fighters and a nine-aircraft detachment of torpedo planes. Ryuho could handle a slightly larger air group of 27 fighters and six torpedo planes.

The standard IJN carrier fighter was the Mitsubishi A6M Type 0 fighter (given the Allied reporting name "Zeke" but most commonly referred to as the Zero). At the start of the war, it was undoubtedly the finest carrier fighter in the world primarily by virtue of its exceptional range and low-

This is a photo of Zuiho from December 1940 following her conversion from a submarine tender. The ship maintained the same basic configuration in June 1944 with the addition of more 25mm antiaircraft guns and radar. The Japanese considered her a useful light carrier conversion with a speed of 28 knots and the capacity to carry 30 aircraft. She was a veteran carrier, being present at the carrier battles of Midway and Santa Cruz, and was not sunk until Leyte Gulf in October 1944. (Yamato Museum)

speed maneuverability. The 1944 version was the A6M5, which had augmented thrust and a slightly higher speed than earlier versions. Compared to the Hellcat, it was well behind in armament, protection, high-altitude performance and higher-speed maneuverability. The IJN's inability to deliver an updated carrier fighter to replace the Zero was a tremendous disadvantage.

The IJN called its dive-bombers "carrier bombers." The standard carrier bomber at the start of the war was the Aichi D3A1 Type 99 (later given the reporting name "Val" by the Allies). The Val looked antiquated with its fixed landing gear, but in the hands of a well-trained pilot it was a very capable dive-bomber. In fall 1942, an improved version, the D3A2, was introduced which had a top speed of 232 knots, but this did not alter the fact that the aircraft was slow and vulnerable to USN fighters. The Val was not the equal of the Dauntless, being less rugged and unable to carry as heavy a bomb load. The replacement for the Val was the Yokosuka D4Y (Allied reporting name "Judy"). This aircraft was introduced in 1942 and was a great improvement over the Val with a top speed of 313 knots and the ability to carry a slightly greater bomb load.

ABOVE LEFT
Chitose pictured in August 1943 following her conversion from a seaplane carrier. This resulted in a ship capable of 29 knots and with the capacity to embark 30 aircraft which made her useful for fleet work. The ship survived Operation *A-Go* without damage but was sunk in October 1944 at Leyte Gulf. (Yamato Museum)

ABOVE RIGHT
Chiyoda was also converted from a seaplane carrier and had the same characteristics as *Chitose*. This December 1943 view shows the relatively austere nature of her conversion. Damaged at Philippine Sea, the light carrier returned to service and was sunk four months later at Leyte Gulf. (Yamato Museum)

The standard IJN fighter during the battle was the A6M5 Zero, which had an improved engine configuration resulting in a slightly greater maximum speed. The improvement was insufficient to deal with modern American fighters like the F6F Hellcat meaning that the Zero was unable to perform in its primary role. This aircraft, captured from the Japanese on Saipan, was photographed on September 25, 1944. Earlier versions of the Zero were employed during the battle as fighter-bombers and could carry a 550-pound bomb. (Naval History and Heritage Command)

The IJN called its torpedo planes "carrier attack planes." Like the USN's Avenger, IJN attack aircraft could perform as torpedo planes and conventional bombers. The standard early-war IJN attack plane was the Nakajima B5N2 Type 97 (reporting name "Kate"). At the time, the Kate was the best torpedo plane in the world and was indirectly responsible for the destruction of three USN fleet carriers. The replacement for the Kate was the Nakajima B6N Type Carrier Attack Bomber (reporting name "Jill"). The Jill experienced several engineering problems during development so was late entering service which required small numbers of Kates to remain in front-line service into mid-1944. The Jill did not turn out to be much of an improvement over its predecessor, except for a slightly improved maximum speed.

The key advantage of Japanese carrier aircraft was their superior range when compared to their American counterparts. This was the result of the lighter construction of Japanese aircraft that in most cases carried little armor and lacked self-sealing fuel tanks. Search range for IJN carrier aircraft extended to some 560nm. The Japanese also held a major advantage in strike range that was normally 300nm. If the Japanese used their air bases in the Marianas, their potential range advantage could be even longer. American commanders greatly feared the potential use of this "shuttle bombing" tactic. Another factor extending the Japanese range advantage was the prevailing winds in the Central Pacific in June 1944. These were easterly trade winds, which meant that the Japanese could approach from the west while moving into the wind allowing them to launch and recover aircraft while headed toward the USN. The Japanese plan to use the superior striking range of their carrier aircraft was the only part of their defensive scheme built on a solid foundation. If he was careful and received timely reports of TF 58's movements, Ozawa could stay beyond the range of USN carrier strikes.

Training

The entire Japanese plan was undermined by the perilous state of training of their aircrews, especially the carrier aircrews. Imperial Japanese Navy naval aviation started the war with the most finely trained pilots in the world. These men achieved a series of victories and fought the USN carrier force to a draw in 1942. However, the attrition of the four carrier battles of 1942, followed by the continuing wastage in the Solomons campaign when the Japanese often used their carrier aircraft from land bases exposing them to further loss, meant that IJN carrier aircrews were but a shadow of their former selves. This meant greatly reduced capabilities in air combat and maritime strike. Skills such as communications and use of radar were also weak.

The air groups of Carrier Division 1, the IJN's premier unit, had only six months' training. The pilots of Carrier Division 3 had only three months. The condition of training for pilots in Carrier Division 2 was even worse with only 100 hours of training. The state of training could not be addressed while the fleet sat at anchor at Tawi-Tawi because the Japanese could not operate out of the protected anchorage owing to the American submarine threat and the need to conserve fuel. The result was that the carrier air groups could not train, which meant that the skills of the neophyte pilots remained low and even the skills of the more advanced pilots atrophied. In addition to the deplorable state of training, maintenance personnel were inexperienced which meant that the state of aircraft maintenance was poor.

An indication of the state of training can be gleaned by an incident on June 13 when a Jill, considered a "hot" aircraft with a high landing speed, crashed on carrier *Taiho* while trying to land. The Jill hit another plane on deck, and before the resulting flames were extinguished, two Jills, two Judys and two Zeros were destroyed.

The Type 97 Carrier Attack Bomber B5N2 Model 12 was the IJN's standard torpedo bomber at the start of the war. Armed with the reliable Type 91 torpedo, it proved a devastating weapon and was indirectly responsible for the loss of three USN fleet carriers. By 1944, it was obsolescent but had to continue in service until its replacement was available in large numbers. During the battle of Philippine Sea it was used almost exclusively in a scouting role. This is a B5N2 from *Zuikaku* in 1943. (Juzo Nakamura via LRA)

Fleet air defense

The IJN recognized that its carriers were vulnerable to enemy attack. Fighter direction was hampered by poor radar and radio performance that limited the ability of controllers to direct airborne fighters. This meant that Japanese CAP was limited to interception over or very close to their

The replacement for the pre-war Type 97 Carrier Attack Bomber was the Nakajima Navy Carrier Attack Bomber B6N2 Tenzan (Heavenly Mountain) Model 12 (Allied reporting name "Jill"). It introduced no major aerodynamic improvements over the earlier aircraft, but did have an engine that produced 80 percent more power resulting in an increased top speed of 299mph. This is a Jill, still with its torpedo onboard, seen from light carrier *Monterey* off Truk probably during the April 30 raid. (Naval History and Heritage Command)

carriers. Imperial Japanese Navy antiaircraft weaponry and fire control was inferior to comparable USN systems. The standard Japanese long-range antiaircraft gun was the Type 89 5in./40. Though an adequate weapon, it was dependent on the Type 94 director which was unable to track fast targets. Unlike USN antiaircraft doctrine that called for aimed fire, IJN doctrine used generally ineffective barrage fire.

The IJN had even bigger issues with its standard Type 96 25mm antiaircraft gun which served in both an intermediate and short-range role. The Type 96 was not effective in either role since it could not track or engage high-speed targets, possessed excessive vibration and muzzle blast which affected accuracy, and was unable to maintain high rates of fire because of the requirement to constantly change small magazines. Against the Helldiver and Avenger, the small (.6 pound) projectile fired by the Type 96 often made little impact. Overall, IJN antiaircraft capabilities were unable to protect surface ships from the increasing weight of USN air attack. This meant that the most effective form of defense was the maneuvering skills of the ship's captain.

Land-based air forces

Perhaps the most important part of the Japanese plan to defend the Marianas was their land-based air forces. The Base Air Force had four air flotillas assigned to it. Each flotilla had a variable number of air groups. These were usually assigned a single type of aircraft to ease maintenance and support requirements. At full strength, these units would have totaled 1,290 aircraft. The problem for the Japanese was that these units were badly under-strength, poorly deployed and suffered from poor serviceability rates.

Japanese sources indicate that only 454 aircraft were available to the Base Air Force in early June and deployed outside Japan. Of these, only 146 were positioned on the Marianas. A significant proportion was deployed on Yap Island (69 aircraft) and Peleliu (105 aircraft) reflecting the Japanese desire to have the upcoming decisive battle occur there. Almost 100 aircraft remained in or near northwestern New Guinea in response to the American invasion of Biak Island. Some 150 aircraft were available in Japan.

Supporting the Base Air Force was a network of air bases that were within range of the battle area. The Japanese had two airfields on Guam with two more under construction, one on Rota, four on Tinian, three on Saipan in addition to one seaplane base, and one on Pagan with another under construction. The one on Pagan was used only to stage aircraft. Each of these airfields, except for one on Saipan, could handle 48 aircraft.

Other airfields on the fringe of the battle area included one on Iwo Jima and one on Chichi Jima. These were important since they allowed the Japanese to stage aircraft from the Home Islands to the Marianas. One airfield was active on Marcus Island. Truk was still usable and had 29 aircraft in early June.

The units of the Base Air Force suffered the same problems as the carrier-based air groups. Training levels were low and basic skills were lacking. Simply transferring aircraft to another base meant that many would never arrive. Facilities on the various island airfields were often primitive, adding to the difficulties of the maintenance personnel who were often inexperienced. All of this combined to create low serviceability rates. Malaria was common on these islands, affecting ground personnel and aircrews.

Before the battle, the Base Air Force was engaged in other battles that caused severe attrition. In particular, the 23rd Air Flotilla suffered heavy losses when it was committed to counter the Allied landing on Biak Island off the northwestern coast of New Guinea. When the battle began, the bulk of the 61st Air Flotilla was on the Marianas. This under-strength unit faced TF 58 alone in the initial phase of the battle and was quickly neutralized.

Aircraft assigned to the Base Air Force were dominated by the Zero, used in both fighter and fighter-bomber roles. Strike aircraft were mainly Judy dive-bombers and a mix of longer-range bombers. These included the Mitsubishi G4M1/2 Type 1 Attack Bomber (reporting name "Betty") which was still the IJN's standard long-range bomber in mid-1944 in spite of the aircraft's shocking vulnerability to interception. This forced the IJN to operate the Betty in a night-attack role. The bomber had an impressive range of up to 3,270nm and could carry bombs or torpedoes. Small numbers of the newer Yokosuka P1Y (reporting name "Frances") bomber was also in service. Its higher speed and superior survivability allowed the IJN to use it in a daytime role.

Surface combatants

In three of the four other carrier battles of the war, the IJN possessed a marked advantage in surface firepower. This translated to a desire to close with the USN carrier task force and finish it off in a surface engagement. This superior firepower did not exist in the case of the Philippine Sea encounter despite the large number of Japanese combatants employed to escort the carriers. Five of the IJN's nine surviving battleships were present, including the two superbattleships *Yamato* and *Musashi*. These possessed the largest (18.1in.) guns ever fitted to a battleship and were well protected, but possessed only a small range advantage over USN's 16in. battleship guns and mounted much inferior fire-control equipment. The other battleships present were *Nagato*, laid down in 1917 but modernized between 1934 and 1936; the ship carried 16in. guns but was relatively slow with a maximum speed of 25 knots. *Kongo* and *Haruna* were both originally launched in 1913 and

Kongo photographed in 1936 after her second reconstruction. Originally designed as battlecruisers, the four ships of the Kongo class were modernized between the wars but still retained a light scale of protection for a battleship. They were used extensively as carrier escorts during war because of their high speed of 30 knots. Both surviving ships, *Kongo* and *Haruna*, were present at Philippine Sea with *Haruna* being damaged. (Yamato Museum)

Heavy cruiser *Mogami* underway on an undetermined date early in the battle. *Mogami* was converted into an aircraft cruiser following damage at Midway and could carry as many as 11 Jake floatplanes. Use of floatplanes from battleships and carriers was an important part of IJN carrier warfare doctrine and was very successful at Philippine Sea. (Yamato Museum)

1915, respectively, as battlecruisers before being modernized twice between 1927 and 1936. These ships carried 14in. main guns and were not well protected by battleship standards.

The IJN brought 11 heavy cruisers to the fight, and these were heavily armed with 8in. main batteries and between 12 and 16 torpedo tubes with reloads. They had proved themselves formidable ships in several clashes earlier in the war. The two modern light cruisers were designed as destroyer leaders and were not heavily armed or protected. By mid-1944, the IJN could only allocate 27 fleet destroyers to the decisive engagement. The IJN saw this as a major disadvantage since these ships with their heavy torpedo batteries were essential components in a surface engagement. In fact, IJN destroyers were superb torpedo boats, but were not as proficient in antisubmarine or antiair screening duties. The number of destroyers was totally inadequate to provide antisubmarine screening for the First Mobile Fleet as was demonstrated during the battle.

Logistical support

The IJN had nothing comparable to the USN's at-sea support capabilities. Only fuel could be provided to the First Mobile Force while underway. If the fleet needed more ammunition or replacement aircraft, it would have to return to a secure anchorage or base. Even fuel was a problem by 1944. Japanese tanker losses at the hands of American submarines had been heavy which limited the amount of fuel available in the forward areas. There was a severe shortage of refined oil products. This shortage was so severe that the IJN lacked the range to engage the Americans around the Marianas. This basic problem was addressed in early May when the Japanese lifted the requirement that all fuel had to be processed. When the First Mobile Fleet moved to Tawi-Tawi, it was only 180 miles from Tarakan, Borneo. The Tarakan fields produced a light oil which could be burned in ship's boilers without refining. However, burning this oil with its heavy sulfur content could damage boilers and posed a serious risk in combat because of its high volatility. With all the First Mobile Fleet's warships and tankers topped up with Tarakan crude, the IJN could give battle in the Marianas.

Unlike the USN, which gave a high priority to logistics and had the resources to build a comprehensive fleet support system, the IJN ran its logistics on a shoestring. For the sortie into the Philippine Sea, the IJN assembled six oilers and organized them into two supply groups. While the USN had the capability to maintain a huge invasion fleet for as long as necessary off the Marianas, the IJN was capable of only sporadic sorties. It is important to note that, even if the Japanese had achieved some level of success in the battle of the Philippine Sea, they did not have the capability to follow up that success. It would have taken weeks to build up enough fuel for another major fleet sortie, find replacement aircraft, and repair and re-provision ships. The IJN was reduced to a raiding force by this point in the war, and was not able to project power on a sustained basis.

Submarines

The IJN's submarine force supported the decisive battle as best it could by sending some 25 subs into action. Many were deployed into scouting and patrol lines, a tactic which had proven faulty since Midway. The "NA" line was deployed in two lines north of the Admiralty Islands supported by two larger I-boats deployed north of New Ireland. Of the ten smaller RO-type boats deployed on the NA line, five were destroyed in late May, four by a single USN destroyer escort. Admiral Takagi ordered three I-boats to move east of Saipan between June 14 and 16, but these were all destroyed by July 4. Overall, Japanese submarines were a non-factor in the battle while recording no successes. For their troubles, 17 IJN subs were lost during the Marianas campaign.

Imperial Japanese Navy destroyers were deficient in antiair warfare, with the exception of the 12-ship Akizuki class. These were designed to escort carriers and were equipped with the excellent Type 98 3.9in. dual-purpose gun. Four were present at Philippine Sea and assigned to escort the fleet carriers of Force A. (Naval History and Heritage Command)

ORDERS OF BATTLE

UNITED STATES NAVY

FIFTH FLEET
ADMIRAL SPRUANCE IN HEAVY CRUISER *INDIANAPOLIS*

Task Force 58   Vice Admiral Mitscher in carrier *Lexington*

Task Group 58.1   Rear Admiral Clark in carrier *Hornet*
Carriers
Hornet

Air Group 2	1 TBM-1C (Avenger)
VB-2 (Bombing Squadron)	33 SB2C-1C (Helldiver)
VF-2 (Fighter Squadron)	36 F6F-3 (Hellcat)
VT-2 (Torpedo Squadron)	18 TBM/TBF-1C
VF(N)-76 (Night fighter Det.)	4 F6F-3N

Yorktown

Air Group 1	1 F6F-3
VB-1	40 SB2C-1C, 4 SBD-5 (Dauntless)
VF-1	41 F6F-3
VT-1	17 TBM/TBF-1C
VF(N)-77 (Detachment)	4 F6F-3N

Belleau Wood

Air Group 24	
VF-24	26 F6F-3
VT-24	9 TBM/TBF-1C

Bataan

Air Group 50	
VF-50	24 F6F-3
VT-50	9 TBM-1C

Heavy cruisers *Baltimore, Boston, Canberra*
Light cruisers *San Juan, Oakland*
Destroyers *Izard, Charrette, Conner, Bell, Burns, Boyd, Bradford, Brown, Cowell, Maury, Craven, Gridley, Helm, McCall*

Task Group 58.2 Rear Admiral Montgomery in carrier *Bunker Hill*
Carriers
Bunker Hill

Air Group 8	1 F6F-3
VB-8	33 SB2C-1C
VF-8	37 F6F-3
VT-8	18 TBM/TBF-1C
VF(N)-76 (Detachment)	4 F6F-3N

Wasp

Air Group 14	1 F6F-3
VB-14	32 SB2C-1C
VF-14	34 F6F-3
VT-14	18 TBM/TBF-1C
VF(N)-76 (Detachment)	4 F6F-3N

Monterey

Air Group 28	
VF-28	21 F6F-3
VT-28	8 TBM-1C

Cabot

Air Group 31	
VF-31	24 F6F-3
VT-31	9 TBF/TBM-1C

Light cruisers *Santa Fe, Mobile, Biloxi*
Destroyers *Owen, Miller, The Sullivans, Stephen Potter, Tingey, Hickox, Hunt, Lewis Hancock, Marshall, Macdonough, Dewey, Hull*

Task Group 58.3   Rear Admiral Reeves in carrier *Enterprise*
Carriers
Enterprise

Air Group 10	
VB-10	21 SBD-5
VF-10	31 F6F-3
VT-10	14 TBM/TBF-1C
VF(N)-101 (Detachment)	3 F4U-2 (Corsair)

Lexington

Air Group 16	1 F6F-3
VB-16	34 SBD-5
VF-16	37 F6F-3
VT-16	17 TBF-1C
VF(N)-76 (Detachment)	4 F6F-3N

San Jacinto

Air Group 51	
VF-51	24 F6F-3
VT-51	8 TBF/TBM-1C

Princeton

Air Group 27	
VF-27	24 F6F-3
VT-27	9 TBM-1C

Heavy cruiser *Indianapolis*
Light cruisers *Cleveland, Montpelier, Birmingham, Reno*
Destroyers *Clarence K. Bronson, Cotton, Dortch, Gatling, Healy, Caperton, Cogswell, Ingersoll, Knapp, Anthony, Wadsworth, Terry, Braine*

Task Group 58.4   Rear Admiral Harrill in carrier *Essex*
Carriers
Essex

Air Group 15	1 F6F-3
VB-15	36 SB2C-1C
VF-15	38 F6F-3
VT-15	15 TBF-1C
VF(N)-77 (Detachment)	4 F6F-3N

Langley

Air Group 32	
VF-32	23 F6F-3
VT-32	9 TBF/TBM-1C

Cowpens

Air Group 25	
VF-25	23 F6F-3
VT-25	9 TBM-1C

Light cruisers *Vincennes, Houston, Miami, San Diego*
Destroyers *Lansdowne, Lardner, McCalla, Case, Lang, Sterrett, Wilson, Ellet, Charles Ausburne, Stanly, Dyson, Converse, Spence, Thatcher*

Task Group 58.7   Vice Admiral Lee in battleship *Washington*
Battleships *Washington, North Carolina, South Dakota, Indiana, Alabama, Iowa, New Jersey*
Heavy cruisers *New Orleans, Minneapolis, San Francisco, Wichita*
Destroyers *Mugford, Patterson, Bagley, Conyngham, Selfridge, Halford, Guest, Bennett, Fullam, Hudson, Twining, Monssen, Yarnall, Stockham*

Task Force 17　　　Vice Admiral Lockwood

Deployed near Bonin Islands: *Plunger, Gar, Archerfish, Plaice, Swordfish*
Deployed near Formosa: *Pintado, Pilotfish, Tunny*
Deployed west of Marianas: *Albacore, Seawolf, Bang, Finback, Stingray*
Deployed near Philippines and Ulithi: *Flying Fish, Muskallunge,*
　　Seahorse, Pipefish, Cavalla, Growler

Seventh Fleet Submarines　　　Rear Admiral R. W. Christie
Deployed southeast of Mindaao: *Hake, Bashaw, Paddle*
Deployed near Tawi-Tawi: *Harder, Haddo, Redfin, Bluefish*
Deployed near Luzon: *Jack, Flier*

Long-Range Aircraft
Seaplane Tender *Ballard* with 5 PBM-5 Mariners from Patrol
　　Squadron 16

IMPERIAL JAPANESE NAVY

First Mobile Fleet　Vice Admiral Ozawa on carrier *Taiho* as of June 19, 1944

Force A　　　　　　　　　　　　　Vice Admiral Ozawa
Carrier Division 1 embarking Air Group 601
Taiho

Fighter Unit	20 A6M5 Zero
Bomber Unit	27 D4Y1 Judy, 1 D3A2 Val
Attack Unit	13 B6N1 Jill
Scout Detachment	3 D4Y1-C Judy

Shokaku

Fighter Unit	34 A6M5
Bomber Unit	18 D4Y1, 3 D3A2
Attack Unit	9 B6N2
Scout Unit	9 D4Y1C, 3 B6N2 (radar-equipped)

Zuikaku

Fighter Unit	24 A6M5
Fighter-bomber Unit	11 A6M2
Bomber Unit	18 D4Y1, 3 D3A2
Attack Unit	15 B6N1
Scout Detachment	2 D4Y1C, 2 B6N2 (radar-equipped)

Heavy cruisers *Myoko* (1 E13A Jake), *Haguro* (1 E13A)
Light cruiser *Yahagi* (2 E13A)
Destroyers *Asagumo, Urakaze, Isokaze, Hatsuyuki, Wakatsuki, Akizuki,*
　　Shimotsuki

Force B　　　　　　　　　　　　Rear Admiral Joshima
Carrier Division 2 embarking Air Group 652
Junyo

Fighter Unit	18 A6M5
Fighter-bomber Unit	9 A6M2
Bomber Unit	11 D4Y1, 9 D3A2 Val
Attack Unit	5 B6N1

Hiyo

Fighter Unit	17 A6M5
Fighter-bomber Unit	9 A6M2
Bomber Unit	19 D3A2
Attack Unit	5 B6N1

Ryuho

Fighter Unit	18 A6M5
Fighter-bomber Unit	9 A6M2
Attack Unit	5 B6N1 Battleship *Nagato* (2 E13A)

Heavy cruiser *Mogami* (5 E13A)
Destroyers *Michishio, Nowaki, Yamagumo, Shigure, Hamakaze,*
　　Hayashimo, Akishimo

Force C　　　　　　　Vice Admiral Kurita in heavy cruiser *Atago*
Carrier Division 3 embarking Air Group 653
Chitose

Fighter Unit	6 A6M5
Fighter-bomber Unit	15 A6M2
Attack Unit	3 B6N1 (Pathfinder), 6 B5N2 Kate (Search)

Chiyoda

Fighter Unit	6 A6M5
Fighter-bomber Unit	15 A6M2
Attack Unit	3 B6N1 (Pathfinder), 6 B5N2 (Search)

Zuiho

Fighter Unit	6 A6M5, 1 A6M2
Fighter-bomber Unit	15 A6M2
Attack Unit	3 B6N1 (Pathfinder), 5 B5N2 (Search)

Battleships *Yamato* (1 E13A, 2 F1M Pete), *Musashi* (1 E13A, 2 F1M
　　Pete), *Kongo* (2 E13A), *Haruna* (2 E13A)
Heavy cruisers *Atago* (2 E13A), *Takao* (2 E13A), *Maya* (2 E13A), *Chokai*
　　(2 E13A), *Kumano* (3 E13A), *Suzuya* (3 E13A), *Tone* (5 E13A),
　　Chikuma (5 E13A)
Light cruiser *Noshiro* (2 E13A)
Destroyers *Shimakaze, Asashimo, Kishinami, Okinami, Tamanami,*
　　Fujinami, Hamanami

1st Supply Force
Oilers *Hayasui, Nichiei Maru, Kokuyo Maru, Seiyo Maru*
Light cruiser *Natori*
Destroyers *Hibiki, Hatsushimo, Yunagi, Tsuga*

2nd Supply Force
Oilers *Genyo Maru, Azusa Maru*
Destroyers *Yukikaze, Uzuki*

Sixth Fleet　　　　　Vice Admiral Takagi on Saipan

*I-5, I-10, I-26, I-38, I-41, I-53, I-184, I-185 RO-36, RO-41, RO-42, RO-43,
　　RO-44, RO-47, RO-68, RO-104, RO-105, RO-106, RO-108, RO-109,
　　RO-112, RO-113, RO-114, RO-115, RO-116, RO-117*

Base Air Force　　　Vice Admiral Kakuta on Tinian

All strengths as of June 3, 1944 unless otherwise indicated.
All aircraft are indicated by their Allied reporting names.
　　7 Jake (7 operational) at Saipan

61st Air Flotilla
121st Air Group
　　8 Judy (5 operational) at Tinian Airfield No. 1
　　5 George fighters (2 operational) at Tinian No. 1
　　4 Judy (2 operational) at Peleliu
261st Air Group
　　25 Zero (A6M5) (18 operational), 1 Zero (A6M3) (1 operational)
　　　at Saipan
　　19 Zero (16 operational) at Saipan
263rd Air Group
　　6 Zero (2 operational) at Guam
　　25 Zero (25 operational) at Peleliu
　　12 Zero (12 operational) at Yokosuka
265th Air Group
　　10 Zeros (1 operational) at Saipan No.1
　　32 Zeros (32 operational) at Yap
321st Air Group
　　14 Irving night fighters (10 operational) at Tinian No. 2
　　6 Irving night fighters (6 operational) at Yap
　　3 Irving night fighters (2 operational) at Tinian No. 1
343rd Air Group
　　14 Zero (5 operational) at Tinian No. 1
　　37 Zero (37 operational) at Peleliu

521st Air Group
  26 Frances bombers (23 operational) Iwo Jima and Japan
  8 Frances (8 operational) at Guam
  18 Frances (17 operational) at Peleliu
  16 Frances (16 operational) at Yap
523rd Air Group
  20 Judy (14 operational) at Tinian No. 2
  21 Judy (21 operational) at Peleliu
  8 Judy (8 operational) at Yap
761st Air Group
  11 Betty bombers (8 operational) at Tinian No. 1
  11 Betty (11 operational) at Peleliu
1021st Air Group
  38 various transports (26 operational) located at Tinian No. 1
  and Japan

22nd Air Flotilla
151st Air Group
  2 land-based recon (possibly Myrt) (1 operational) at Truk
  Harujima
202nd Air Group
  43 Zero (42 operational) at Wasile
  3 Zero (2 operational) at Yap
251st Air Group
  5 Irving (4 operational) at Truk Takeshima
253rd Air Group
  31 Zero (24 operational) at Truk Takeshima
301st Air Group
  52 Zero (47 operational) at Yokosuka
  60 Jack fighters (40 operational) at Yokosuka (number located in
  Japan unknown as of June 1)

503rd Air Group
  14 Judy (14 operational) at Wasile
  4 Judy (none operational) at Yap
551st Air Group
  1 Jill (none operational) at Truk Kadeshima
  7 Kate (3 operational) at Truk Kadeshima
755th Air Group
  12 Betty (7 operational) at Guam No. 1
  11 Betty (9 operational) at Truk Harujima

26th Air Flotilla
201st Air Group
  12 Zero (12 operational) at Cebu (40 Zero in process of
  transferring from Japan on 21 June)
501st Air Group
  1 Zero (1 operational); 14 Zero at Aparri on June 21 transferring
  from Japan
  3 Judy (1 operational) at Davao
  1 Val at Davao
751st Air Group
  11 Betty (10 operational) at Davao

23rd Air Flotilla
153rd Air Group
  2 Judy reconnaissance aircraft (none operational) at Kendari (as
  of June 10)
  19 Zero (16 operational) at Kendari (as of June 10)
732nd Air Group
  12 Betty (9 operational) at Wasile (as of June 1)
753rd Air Group
  2 Betty (2 operational) at Kendari
  3 Betty at Sorong and 2 on Degos (as of June 10)

OPPOSING PLANS

THE AMERICAN PLAN

The invasion of the Marianas promised to be a major event in the war to defeat Japan. The capture of the islands accelerated the pace of the American advance across the Central Pacific and brought the potential power of the Army Air Force's strategic bombers within range of Japan. Given this, the Americans were confident that the IJN would give battle in a major engagement. This presented the USN with the possibility of inflicting a major defeat on the IJN which had been avoiding such a battle for 20 months.

Admiral Nimitz issued the invasion plan for the Marianas on April 23, 1944. The codename for the largest American naval operation of the war was Operation *Forager*. The plan called for the initial seizure of the islands in the southern Marianas with a D-Day of June 15. Admiral Spruance had the primary mission of conducting the invasion and defeating any Japanese naval reaction. Admiral William F. Halsey's Third Fleet, operating in the South Pacific, as well as Lockwood's submarines, were ordered to support Spruance's operations.

Based on Nimitz's campaign plan for Operation *Forager*, Spruance issued his plan on May 12, 1944. The Fifth Fleet's mission was to capture Saipan, Tinian and Guam while being ready to "drive off or destroy enemy forces attempting to interfere with the movement to or the landing operations at each objective." D-Day was the landing on Saipan with the landings on the other two islands to take place later.

Task Force 58 was tasked with neutralizing Japanese air power with the range to attack the invasion force prior to the landing in Saipan. The Americans understood that long-range air strikes from land-based Japanese aircraft formed an essential part of the Japanese plan and offered the IJN the only real possibility of weakening the American fast carrier force before the outnumbered First Mobile Force was committed to action.

On June 12, TF 58 would strike air bases and other targets on Saipan, Tinian, Guam and the smaller Mariana Islands of Rota and Pagan. These strikes would continue the following day to render Japanese airfields on those islands inoperable. Battleships and other warships from TF 58 would conduct operations to suppress Japanese coastal batteries and shell defensive positions on Saipan and Tinian. By June 14, it was expected that TF 58 would have gained air control over the Marianas and would be on-call for air support missions as required. Two of TF 58's carrier groups, TGs 58.1 and 58.4, would head toward Iwo and Chichi Jima to strike airfields used by the Japanese to stage aircraft into the Marianas.

On the day of the landings, June 15, TGs 58.2 and 58.3 were tasked with maintaining air control over the Marianas and supporting the landings as required. Following the landings, TF 58 would replenish with fuel and aircraft and continue operations to maintain air control. Task Force 58 would remain in position to the west of the Marianas ready to respond to any counterattack by the IJN.

Lockwood's submarines were to support the entire operation. His plan, issued on May 21, ordered 19 submarines to deploy in support of the invasion. These included five off the Bonin Islands, three in the western Philippine Sea, five near the Marianas, five near the Philippines and one off the Surigao Strait.

The 7th Fleet deployed nine more submarines – three southeast of Mindanao, four off Tawi-Tawi and two off Luzon. The submarines were responsible for performing reconnaissance of IJN fleet movements, conducting attacks when the opportunities presented themselves and rescuing downed USN aircrews.

Before going into detail on the Japanese plan, it is important to explore what the state of USN intelligence was in mid-1944. In general, the Americans possessed a significant intelligence advantage over the Japanese during this portion of the war. Before the battle, USN intelligence arrived at an IJN order of battle that was very close to ground truth. It understood that the state of training for the IJN's carrier aviators was not advanced. The Americans expected the First Mobile Fleet to contest an invasion of the Marianas. Tactically, they expected the Japanese to prefer a night action and for the Japanese carriers to strike from unexpected directions and conduct a flank attack. This was not based solely on signals intelligence or on previous Japanese operational tendencies, but on an extraordinary source which fell into Allied hands on April 3, 1944. This occurred when the then commander of the Combined Fleet, Admiral Koga, and his staff were moving by flying boat from Palau to Davao in the southern Philippines. Of the three aircraft, Koga's disappeared in a storm and a second crashed on March 31 with the staff officers aboard falling into the hands of Philippine guerrillas. In their possession was Combined Fleet Secret Order No. 73, dated March 8, 1944. This was the "Z" Plan which outlined Japanese intentions for a decisive battle in the Central Pacific. The plan was recovered by a Filipino and was transferred by USN submarine to Australia. It was translated and in the hands of major Allied commands by the end of the month. It was assessed to represent a valid representation of how the Japanese would conduct an operation in the Central Pacific when the invasion of the Marianas got underway.

Assessment of the USN plan for Operation Forager

By this point in the war, USN operational planning was solid since it was based on a growing body of experience and success. The plan to take the Marianas reflected the USN's operational maturity. The extensive pre-landing operations to neutralize Japanese land-based air power based in the Marianas and to restrict the flow of aircraft into the fight was key to the coming battle. The elimination of Japanese land-based airpower in the region unhinged the entire Japanese plan and reduced the battle to a carrier engagement with the outnumbered First Mobile Fleet that the Americans were sure they could defeat. The only potential problem was that Spruance appeared to give precedence to guarding the invasion force over destroying the Japanese fleet. He feared a Japanese flanking attack against the invasion force as called for in the captured Z Plan. When faced with the dilemma during the battle of aggressively going after the First Mobile Fleet or hanging back and ensuring the invasion force was protected, he elected to fight a defensive battle.

THE JAPANESE PLAN

Even in 1944, the IJN retained the notion that the war could be decided in a single decisive battle. This was the underlying theme of Japanese preparations leading to the battle of the Philippine Sea. This notion, a constant in IJN naval planning, was re-emphasized in September 1943 when the Combined Fleet again issued a policy that the entire Combined Fleet was to seek a decisive battle against the USN. Imperial General Headquarters planned for this in mid-1944 in response to American attacks in the Central Pacific or the Philippines. Planning for this latest decisive battle began in August 1943 as part of what Admiral Koga called the "Third Phase Operations of the War."

The IJN's part of this overall scheme was the Z Plan. It was originally put together in August 1943 by Koga and his staff and called for the Combined Fleet to fight a decisive battle against the USN. Operating from Truk, the Combined Fleet would defend strategic areas designated by Imperial General Headquarters by giving battle in "interception zones" which were centered on an advanced base. These interception zones were divided into first, second and third zones of defense. The design of this interlocking system of defense was to have bases with airfields about 300nm apart. The Marianas were in the third zone of defense with the first zone in the Marshalls and Gilberts.

The key role in this scheme was played by the Combined Fleet as it was the mobile reserve to come to the rescue of any base under attack. The Japanese had plans to respond to any Allied incursion from the Kurile Islands in the Northern Pacific to as far south as Western New Guinea, but they foresaw the main operation was likely to occur in the Central Pacific. Here they could fight a set-piece battle, much like the pre-war IJN plans to detect, attrite, and then engage the USN in a decisive battle. In the 1943–44 iteration, the Japanese planned to detect the approaching American invasion force with aircraft, submarines and smaller surface combatants. Land-based air defense would come into play and focus on the USN's carrier force to create favorable conditions for attacking the invasion force itself.

At the decisive moment, the First Mobile Fleet would come into action. Tactically, the Z Plan had four sub-plans designated A through D that directed how the First Mobile Fleet would operate in the face of the enemy. These were a combination of air and surface attacks; two of these envisioned surface attacks only, one was a combined air and surface attack operation, and a fourth featured air attacks by carrier and land-based aircraft. In general, the carriers would operate beyond the range of enemy reconnaissance aircraft and then "maneuver to strike the enemy in the flank."

To their credit, Japanese planners were not unaware of potential serious problems with the Z Plan. The biggest were the inadequate state of training for the carrier air units and a general lack of fuel for the Combined Fleet. They believed that by mid-April these problems would be addressed and the operation could be conducted as planned. If fuel or training problems persisted, the actual operation would be conducted by whatever sub-plan A through D was appropriate.

Admiral Koga did not get a chance to put his Z Plan into action since he was killed in an air accident in March 1944. When the Americans invaded the Gilberts and the Marshalls, he decided not to execute the Z Plan since the First Mobile Fleet was unable to successfully intervene because of the low state of aircrew training.

After Koga's death, responsibility for planning the decisive battle fell to Admiral Toyoda. Toyoda kept the Z Plan as the basis of future operations, but did make some minor adjustments. The plan was renamed *A-Go*. In April 1944, the Marianas were designated as an area of national importance that had to be defended. Accordingly, the First Mobile Fleet, all available land-based air units and all submarines were allocated to the decisive battle. There were several keys to the battle. Advance warning of the USN's intentions would be provided by the Base Air Force, which would conduct reconnaissance of all major USN anchorages and bases. Imperial Japanese Navy land-based air units played another key role since it was assumed that at least one third of the USN's carriers would be neutralized before the decisive battle phase. To do this, the Base Air Force was organized into three groups – the 1st Attack Group based in the Marianas; the 2nd on Palau, Yap and Davao; and the 3rd in the Dutch East Indies.

Following the strikes from land-based aircraft, the First Mobile Fleet would make its appearance. The key to its success would be to make large-scale daytime air attacks while operating beyond the range of the aircraft from the USN's carriers. In the decisive phase of the battle, the First Mobile Fleet would cooperate with the Base Air Force to destroy the remaining USN carriers and then set about to destroy the invasion force.

In addition to air attacks, the Japanese still foresaw a major role for surface forces. Preferably, these would be able to attack USN formations at night. The updated January 1944 night-fighting doctrine was based on pre-war night-fighting doctrine in which heavy cruisers and even battleships would destroy USN screening forces to cover the massed torpedo attack of the destroyer squadrons. The priority for attack was the USN carriers, battleships, and then large cruisers. There was also a scenario in which American transports would be attacked.

The period leading up to the execution of *A-Go* gave the IJN opportunity to rehearse it. This occurred in a series of tabletop maneuvers and war games. The first was on Ozawa's flagship *Taiho* on April 27. On May 2, the Naval General Staff oversaw a war game and a staff study on the Combined Fleet's flagship, the light cruiser *Oyodo* anchored in Tokyo Bay, on *Taiho* and on the flagships of smaller units. The game was critiqued the same day and Emperor Hirohito attended the review. *Taiho* was also the scene for more tabletop maneuvers in May. This made *A-Go* the most prepared IJN plan to date.

The final version of *A-Go* was issued on May 3 when Imperial General Headquarters issued Order Number 373, "The Immediate Operational Policy to be Adhered by the Combined Fleet." This, and an accompanying order from the Navy Section to the Combined Fleet, emphasized air operations and surprise. The Base Air Force and the First Mobile Fleet would cooperate to destroy the enemy in a "single blow." Admiral Toyoda's Order Number 76 to the Combined Fleet called for a decisive battle around Palau and the western Carolines. The Base Air Force and the First Mobile Fleet would attack the USN's carrier force. If the American force did not fight the decisive battle in the area desired and showed up off the Marianas instead, it was to be attacked by the Base Air Force and then lured south toward Palau where the decisive daylight battle could be fought. With continuous air, surface and submarine attacks, the Japanese thought they could reduce the USN carrier force's strength enough to give the First Mobile Fleet a real chance of victory.

On May 20, following attacks on Marcus Island by TF 58, the Japanese issued orders to activate *A-Go*. This started the movement of aircraft to the Marianas where they hoped to have everything in place by the end of May.

Assessment of Operation A-Go

By 1944, the IJN was dealing from a position of severe weakness. The *A-Go* plan was like pre-war IJN plans for a decisive battle, but in 1944 the conditions necessary for success simply did not exist. It is debatable if they ever did even when the IJN was at the height of its preparedness before the war. The pillars that *A-Go* depended upon were unsteady at best and already in a state of collapse at worst. The plan depended on the massive application of airpower, and it was here that the Japanese were weakest. The Base Air Force was unable to carry out its reconnaissance duties, allowing the Americans to achieve operational and tactical surprise. This caught the Base Air Force out of position and gave the First Mobile Fleet a late start to intervene in the battle. More disastrously, the Base Air Force was unable to conduct anything like successful attacks against the USN's carriers force, thus undermining a key premise of the plan to inflict severe attrition on the USN. This should not have been a surprise to the Japanese since the ability of the USN's Fast Carrier Task Force to operate within range of Japanese land-based airpower with relative immunity had been demonstrated throughout 1944.

The decisive battle phase was based on a flight of fancy. The Japanese were well aware of the limited capabilities of their carrier aviation units. Besides being outnumbered more than two to one by USN carrier aircraft, the aircrews of the First Mobile Fleet were barely able to perform basic take-off, landing and over-water navigation; their abilities to perform advanced functions like air combat and hitting a maneuvering target at sea were even more suspect. The Japanese were aware of these limitations, but chose to ignore them. Even the notion that the IJN's surface force could overcome its numerical inferiority to beat the USN's surface force in a night engagement was based on an outdated notion from the early-war period when the IJN's night-fighting capabilities were unrivalled. Throughout the Solomons campaign the IJN's night-fighting edge had eroded as the USN successfully learned to employ radar in night actions and to fully exploit the offensive capabilities of its destroyers. The very idea that the USN would allow itself to be caught in a night engagement with the IJN under unfavorable tactical circumstances was ridiculous.

In conclusion, there was very little prospect that *A-Go* would end successfully for the Japanese. The superiority of the USN in all aspects of naval warfare was simply too great by this period of the war.

THE BATTLE

SIDESHOW AT BIAK

One of the reasons for the split American command structure in the Pacific between Nimitz and MacArthur was that an advance on two axes would keep the Japanese off balance. The invasion of Biak Island in the immediate period before the landing on Saipan was one of the few instances where this actually occurred. Biak is a large island off the western tip of New Guinea. In 1943, it was identified as a must-hold spot by the Japanese. If the Americans could build airfields on it, they could strike Palau and make it difficult for Japanese surface forces to conduct *A-Go*.

On May 27, the Americans landed an Army division on the island. The Japanese responded immediately by increasing the strength of the 23rd Air Flotilla, the Base Air Force unit responsible for conducting operations in the area, from 16 to 200 aircraft. These aircraft were drawn from Japan and the Philippines and were the same units earmarked for *A-Go*. The Japanese also planned a counterlanding on Biak codenamed Operation *KON*. Ozawa refused to commit the First Mobile Fleet, so other forces were cobbled together and sent to Davao in the southern Philippines. The first attempt to send reinforcements to the island began on May 31, and by June 3 the Japanese transport unit was spotted and shadowed by American B-24 bombers. The loss of surprise forced Toyoda to cancel the operation later that day.

Another attempt was made starting on June 7. The following day six destroyers carrying troops were attacked by American B-25s; one was sunk and three slightly damaged, but the Japanese pressed on to Biak. An Allied cruiser force detected the Japanese force that night. The Japanese withdrew, and in a two-hour stern chase the remaining destroyers escaped.

Ozawa decided to make another effort to get troops to Biak, and the third effort was planned to be much larger than the first two. To aid the next effort, the superbattleships *Yamato* and *Musashi* were detached from the First Mobile Fleet and sent to take part in *KON*. By the evening of June 11, the forces for the next attempt were assembled at an anchorage in Halmahera. That was the same day that TF 58 aircraft attacked Guam and Saipan. Toyoda suspended *KON* and ordered the battleships to head north to rejoin the First Mobile Fleet. The 23rd Air Flotilla was moved to Palau.

The Biak episode was important for several reasons. In a number of respects, it was a dress rehearsal for *A-Go*. The episode demonstrated the difficulty the Japanese would have in moving a surface force in a timely manner to intervene against an Allied invasion. It proved impossible to do this undetected in the face of Allied intelligence, meaning strategic, operational or even tactical surprise was impossible. Most importantly, it showed the ineffectiveness of the IJN's land-based air power. The Japanese had difficulty massing land-based air power at the point of decision and, once they did, the results were unimpressive. In three attacks against Allied naval forces with no defensive air cover near Biak between June 2 and 4, 129 Japanese aircraft were unable to score a single hit. This was a real indicator of the state of training of the IJN's land-based air units. The Biak episode also resulted in the Base Air Force being out of position when TF 58 showed up off the Marianas on June 11.

FIRST MOVES

The intricate movements of the Marianas invasion began in the last week of May when parts of the invasion fleet departed Hawaii and headed for the main assembly areas in the Marshalls. On June 7, Spruance arrived at Eniwetok in the Marshalls and called all his key commanders together for a final planning conference where he reviewed the plans of his subordinate task force commanders.

Immediately before the battle, TF 58 was at the new fleet anchorage at Majuro. It departed on June 6 and refueled two days later. The battleships of TG 58.7 were reincorporated into the four carrier groups on June 8. Japanese air reconnaissance did provide a basic framework of USN operations: flights over Majuro tracked TF 58 as present on June 5 and a flight on June 9 observed that the carriers formerly present in Majuro had departed. They remained unlocated until two days later when they began air attacks on Guam and Saipan.

Lexington photographed from the back seat of a SBD Dauntless dive-bomber that has just taken off. The aircraft is part of a strike on the Marianas on June 13. (Naval History and Heritage Command)

TF 58 VERSUS THE BASE AIR FORCE

Instead of the planned beginning of strikes on Japanese airfields in the Marianas on June 12, TF 58 initiated operations a day earlier. This was done for several reasons, but primarily to gain surprise since the task force had not been detected as it approached the Marianas. On the morning of the 11th, several Japanese aircraft approaching TF 58 were shot down by CAP. When TF 58 reached a position some 200nm east of Guam, Mitscher launched 208 fighters and eight Avengers to strike airfields on Saipan and Tinian. Intense air opposition was encountered and the Hellcats claimed 86 Japanese aircraft destroyed in the air and another 33 on the ground. The Japanese admitted to losing 36 aircraft. American losses were 11 fighters.

During the early hours of the 12th, TF 58 was attacked by some ten Betty torpedo bombers from Truk that used flares to identify targets in the darkness, but no ships were hit. Later in the day, TG 58.4 conducted strikes against a large Japanese convoy about 160nm northwest of Saipan. American aviators claimed one torpedo boat, three subchasers and ten cargo ships sunk.

Throughout June 12 and 13, three of TF 58's carrier groups continued raids on airfields and other installations on Saipan and Tinian. Activity on the 12th was very heavy with a total of 1,472 combat sorties being recorded. By the end of this period, the Americans assessed that land-based Japanese air power in the Marianas had been neutralized. During the same period, TG 58.1 was busy attacking Guam. The intensity of American air attacks slowed on June 14 and 15 since two carrier groups were moving north to strike Chichi and Iwo Jima and the other two took the opportunity to refuel. Not until the evening of the 15th did the Japanese mount another air attack on TF 58. The first group from Guam was intercepted by CAP from TG 58.3 at dusk. Seven Japanese aircraft were claimed and none got through to the carriers. A larger group from Yap attacked TG 58.3 after sunset and was disrupted by a couple of American night fighters. About a dozen Japanese torpedo bombers actually launched an attack, but no hits were made.

Meanwhile, the battleships of TF 58 proceeded to Saipan and Tinian to conduct a surface bombardment. All seven battleships were used in this effort on June 13, but despite the expenditure of 2,232 16in. and 12,544 5in. shells, the operation was a failure since the ships were unpracticed in the art of conducting shore bombardment. The following day, the ships of the invasion fleet took over bombardment duties releasing the fast battleships to return to the carriers.

Task Groups 58.1 and 58.4 refueled on June 14 and were released that night to head to Chichi and Iwo Jima. The strikes on Japanese airfields located there began on the afternoon of the following day. The Japanese put up a robust defense, but 28 of the 37 Zeros sent to meet the Americans were shot down and another seven destroyed on the ground for the loss

A burning Japanese aircraft, probably a Betty from Truk, crashes astern *Lexington* on the evening of June 15. Despite Japanese planning assumptions that their land-based air forces would destroy a third of TF 58's carriers, they were totally ineffective during the battle. (Naval History and Heritage Command)

of only two American aircraft. Bad weather prevented morning strikes on the 16th, but when the Americans returned to Iwo Jima with 54 aircraft in the afternoon, they found Japanese aircraft lined up on the runway; 63 were claimed, though not confirmed by Japanese sources. Only two American aircraft were lost to antiaircraft and operational causes. Following the afternoon raid, the two task groups turned south to follow orders by Mitscher to be in position off Saipan on the 18th. This excursion proved successful since some 100 Japanese aircraft which could have intervened in the upcoming battle were destroyed.

This view shows D-Day at Saipan with amphibious tractors loaded with Marines headed toward the beach moving past bombarding cruisers. The ship in the background is heavy cruiser *Indianapolis*. Though better known as the ship sunk by a Japanese submarine in July 1945 with a resulting horrific loss of life, the ship spent much of the war as the flagship of the Fifth Fleet with Admiral Spruance embarked. (Naval History and Heritage Command)

Along four miles of beaches, two Marine divisions conducted the landings on Saipan on June 15. Japanese resistance was heavy, but by the end of the day 20,000 Marines were ashore and the beachhead was secure. With the Japanese unable to eliminate the Marines as they landed, the fate of the island's defense was in the hands of the First Mobile Fleet.

On June 16, Mitscher continued strikes against Guam and Tinian. Several Japanese aircraft were destroyed on the ground and in the air, but these airfields remained usable. The following day saw an increase in Japanese air activity. A small strike flown from Truk – five torpedo bombers and one J1N1-S night fighter (Allied reporting name "Irving") – attacked a transport group east of Saipan at 1750hrs. Three Japanese aircraft were claimed as destroyed, but a torpedo hit the small landing craft *LCI-468* that later sank. On June 18, the Japanese mounted a larger raid, this time from Yap Island. This operation featured 31 Zeros, 17 Judys and two P1Y twin-engined bombers (Allied reporting name "Frances"). CAP did not intercept this group before it attacked shipping off the landing beach at Saipan that resulted in damage to a tank landing ship (LST). The attack group then encountered the USN's escort carrier groups and attacked them at dusk. Two escort carriers were near missed and *Fanshaw Bay* was hit by a bomb which penetrated to the hangar deck. The carrier was forced to retire for repairs. As usual, Japanese aviators over-claimed, stating that three or four carriers from TF 58 had been hit.

THE JAPANESE RESPONSE

The appearance of TF 58 off the Marianas on June 11 was a surprise to the Japanese. By the following day, Japanese air reconnaissance provided a fairly accurate depiction of TF 58's strength and location. On the 13th, Toyoda was aware of the bombardment of Saipan and Tinian and the continuing American air attacks on the Marianas. He ordered forces to go on alert to conduct *A-Go* and canceled Operation *KON*. Land-based air forces were ordered to move to the Marianas and the First Mobile Fleet departed Tawi-

Tawi at 1000hrs. Toyoda tentatively set June 19 as the decisive battle day. Accordingly, Ozawa's force moved from Tawi-Tawi to the Guimaras where from 1700hrs on June 14 to 0700hrs on the 15th, it took on supplies.

Reports of the American landing on Saipan reached Toyoda early on the 15th. At 0717hrs he ordered *A-Go* to begin. At 0900hrs, the First Mobile Fleet departed the Guimaras and headed to the northeast. At 1730hrs, the Japanese fleet entered the Philippine Sea through the San Bernardino Strait. The superbattleships *Yamato* and *Musashi* were not with the main body, but were proceeding independently through the Philippine Sea with two heavy cruisers, a light cruiser and five destroyers to join with Ozawa. Once into the Philippine Sea, Ozawa headed southeasterly. At about 1700hrs on the 16th, *Yamato* and *Musashi* joined with the First Mobile Fleet. The Japanese began to refuel which was not completed until 1000hrs on the 17th.

TRACKING THE FIRST MOBILE FLEET

As Ozawa brought his carriers into the Philippine Sea and prepared for battle, the Americans struggled to get a track on his movements. Because the movement of Ozawa's force was conducted under radio silence, and because it was out of range of American search planes, the only way to track it was with submarines. This resulted in a paucity of data for USN intelligence officers and kept Spruance mostly in the dark up until the battle was joined on June 19.

At 1300hrs on June 13, submarine *Redfin* provided the first report on Ozawa's force. The submarine reported sighting four battleships, six carriers, eight cruisers and six destroyers headed north through Sibutu Passage between Borneo and Sulu Archipelago. This was Ozawa leaving Tawi-Tawi. Based on this information, the Japanese could not reach the Marianas until June 17, so Spruance went ahead with the landing on Saipan and the raids on Chichi and Iwo Jima.

Signals intelligence late on the 15th confirmed that a major IJN fleet operation was underway. Though the Americans could not break the internal text of IJN messages, they could learn much from the message externals. These suggested the First Mobile Fleet was intent on contesting the landing on Saipan, but Spruance still had no accurate idea of Ozawa's precise intentions or movements.

At 1835hrs on June 15, the submarine *Flying Fish* reported that a force of Japanese battleships and at least three carriers had passed through the San Bernardino Strait. The sighting report from the submarine was monitored by the Japanese who knew they had been located. About one hour later, at 1945hrs, submarine *Seahorse* sighted a Japanese force 200nm east-southeast of Surigao Strait. The exact composition of this force was unclear, but was thought to be *Yamato* and *Musashi* plus escorts. The submarine was not able to send a signal of its sighting until 0400hrs on June 16. Additionally, throughout the 15th, a growing body of signals intelligence indicated that a major IJN fleet action was underway.

While Spruance and Mitscher groped in the dark, the Japanese had a much better idea of TF 58's strength and movements. Ozawa's staff correctly assessed that TF 58 had 15 carriers, seven fleet and eight converted cruisers. However, they assessed that only ten of these would leave the invasion area and move to the west of the Marianas out to a maximum distance of 300nm.

Movement of Japanese naval forces, June 13–17

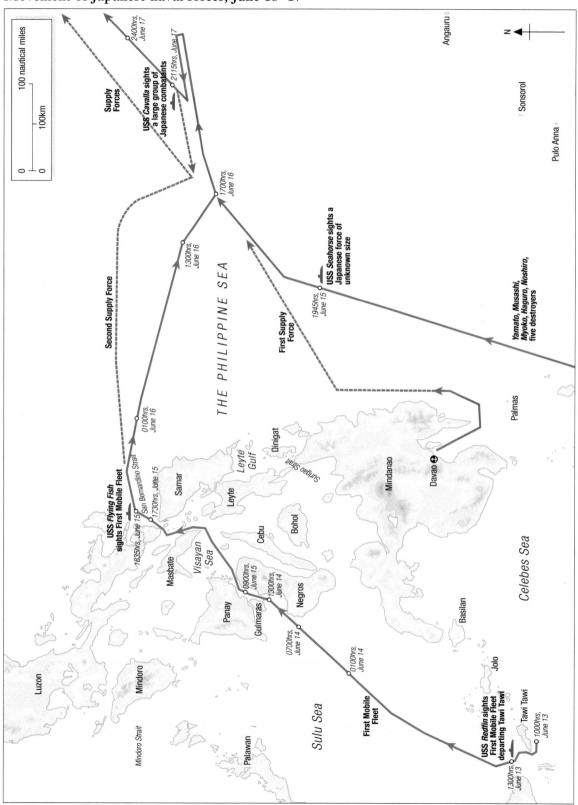

2400hrs, June 17

2115hrs, June 17

Supply Forces

USS *Cavalla* sights a large group of Japanese combatants

Second Supply Force

1700hrs, June 16

1300hrs, June 16

USS *Seahorse* sights a Japanese force of unknown size

1945hrs, June 15

First Supply Force

Yamato, Musashi, Myoko, Haguro, Noshiro, five destroyers

THE PHILIPPINE SEA

0100hrs, June 16

USS *Flying Fish* sights First Mobile Fleet

San Bernardino Strait

1835hrs, June 15

1730hrs, June 15

Leyte Gulf

Dinigat

Leyte

Samar

Masbate

Visayan Sea

Cebu

Bohol

Surigao Strait

Mindanao

Davao

Palmas

0900hrs, June 15

1300hrs, June 14

Panay

Guimaras

Negros

Celebes Sea

Basilan

0700hrs, June 14

0100hrs, June 14

First Mobile Fleet

Jolo

Sulu Sea

Tawi Tawi

1000hrs, June 13

USS *Redfin* sights First Mobile Fleet departing Tawi Tawi

1300hrs, June 13

Luzon

Mindoro

Mindoro Strait

Palawan

Angauru

Sonsorol

Pulo Anna

N

100 nautical miles

100km

0   0

51

They also foresaw American operations to cut off the southern Marianas from air and other reinforcement. Ozawa determined that he must bring the battle to a decisive phase as soon as possible. This meant that it had to occur no later than June 19, and could occur the preceding day depending on Spruance's movements. He selected a battle plan to maximize daylight air attacks. Before the battle was joined, he planned to conduct intensive reconnaissance, especially to the north, to avoid being surprised. Then he would close on TF 58 to launch his attacks.

SPRUANCE PREPARES

With a major carrier battle brewing, Spruance moved the invasion force east of Saipan on June 18, with the exception of 17 LSTs and three other transports, until the battle was over. The day before, Turner sent five heavy cruisers, three light cruisers and 13 destroyers to reinforce TF 58. This left seven battleships, three cruisers (one heavy and two light) and some 13 destroyers both for fire support of the Marines ashore and local defense of the beachhead. The seven remaining escort carriers were assigned to provide air defense for the invasion force that had been ordered east of Saipan.

Mitscher was busy assembling his dispersed task groups for battle. Task Groups 58.1 and 58.4 were returning from their jaunt north to hit Iwo Jima. While returning, they would search to the north and west for Ozawa; additionally, TG 58.1 was ordered to hit targets on Guam and Rota, and TG 58.4 to strike Pagan on June 17. By 1200hrs on June 18, all four task groups would be joined up at a position some 150nm west of Saipan. Prior to that rendezvous, TGs 58.2 and 58.3 searched out to 325nm to the west beginning on 0700hrs on June 17 and found nothing. Earlier in the day, submarine *Cavalla* sighted Ozawa's 2nd Supply Force. Lockwood ordered the submarine to maintain contact, but it was unable to do so.

Also in the afternoon of the 17th, Mitscher directed the seven battleships, four heavy cruisers and 13 destroyers that comprised the battle line to leave the carrier task groups and form TG 58.7. The reduction in the antiaircraft power of each task group was accepted since it would be easier to form the battle line before the battle instead of during it. Spruance envisioned a major role for the battle line in the pursuit phase either taking on the Japanese surface force, should it accept battle, or finishing off cripples from American air strikes.

For another day, Spruance had no locating information on the Japanese carriers.

SPRUANCE'S DECISION

Spruance's first break came at 2115hrs on June 17 when submarine *Cavalla* sighted a large group of Japanese combatants zigzagging at high speed some 700nm west of Guam. The force included 15 combatants, a least one of which was a carrier, but darkness prevented a firm identification. Mitscher did not receive this report until 0345hrs on June 18. During the night of June 17–18, four Martin PBM seaplanes operating from a tender off Saipan made a search out to 600nm but picked up nothing.

When Spruance finally received the spotting report from *Cavalla*, this prompted a decision that turned out to be the most important of the battle. Assuming that the report from *Cavalla* was Ozawa's main force, and assuming it would continue at a speed of 19 knots to the east, Spruance's staff calculated that the Japanese would still be about 500nm from TF 58 at 0530hrs on the 18th. This placed the Japanese well out of range of American searches or strikes. The only way to alter this situation was to steam TF 58 to the southwest toward the contact and plan to locate and engage the Japanese during the afternoon of the 18th.

Mitscher advised the aggressive option of steaming to the southwest to close the range on Ozawa's force. He wanted to launch afternoon strikes to locate and possibly attack Ozawa and even advocated a nighttime surface engagement. While this offered the possibility of opening the battle on terms set by the Americans, there were several problems with it in Spruance's calculating mind. The first was that TF 58 was not yet concentrated; TGs 58.1 and 58.4 were not due to link up with the other two task groups operating west of Saipan until 1200hrs on the 18th. If he allowed Mitscher to take off to the west, it would only be with two task groups. Since the Japanese possessed longer-range strike aircraft, this offered Ozawa the chance to attack TF 58 and defeat it piecemeal. As for the prospects of a night engagement, both Spruance and Lee declined that possibility.

Vice Admiral Mitscher photographed on the bridge of his flagship *Lexington* on June 19. He advocated a much more aggressive approach to dealing with the threat from Ozawa's carriers but was overruled by Spruance. Nevertheless, Mitscher's TF 58 was able to withstand a first Japanese strike with no significant damage. (Naval History and Heritage Command)

The lack of clarity about Ozawa's movements gave Spruance pause and ultimately made him choose a conservative course of action on June 18. He was mindful of the details of the captured *Z* Plan which called for Japanese flank attacks against the invasion force. The only reports available to him so far indicated a force of 15 ships, leaving the bulk of the Japanese fleet unaccounted for.

At 2000hrs, TF 58 changed course toward Saipan. Intense debate ensued among Spruance's staff but, in the end, there was too much uncertainty to allow Spruance to change his mind and place the invasion of Saipan in jeopardy. At 2130hrs, he decided to stay near Saipan and fight a defensive battle on the 19th. A message from Nimitz arrived at 2200hrs relaying the location of Ozawa's force based on direction-finding from a transmission at 2023hrs. At 2346hrs, Spruance copied a message from Lockwood that a report from submarine *Stingray* was unreadable because of jamming by the Japanese who were assumedly in the immediate vicinity of the submarine. *Stingray* was located about 435nm west of Saipan. These latest data points seemed to suggest a movement of the Japanese force to the east.

In a last effort to change Spruance's mind, Mitscher sent him a message at about 2330hrs and proposed a course change to the west at 0130hrs in order to position TF 58 to launch a strike against the Japanese carrier force at 0500hrs. At 0038hrs on the 19th, Spruance sent a message rejecting the proposal. The die was finally cast for a defensive battle on June 19.

OZAWA'S DECISION

Ozawa wanted to initiate decisive operations on the 19th, but realized that the best opportunity might come the day before. As Spruance struggled to gain an understanding of Japanese movements, Ozawa enjoyed a relative wealth of data on the movements of TF 58. At 0600hrs on the 18th, Japanese search floatplanes from the First Mobile Fleet spotted six carriers from TF 58. In the afternoon, seven aircraft from Carrier Division 1 flying out to 420nm spotted TF 58 after its 1200hrs rendezvous. The first report was issued at 1514hrs and included detection of an American task group with two carriers. A second aircraft sighted a task group with an "unknown number of carriers" at 1600hrs and later issued another report at 1710hrs which identified two task groups, each with two carriers. These were within strike range, but Ozawa elected not to launch an immediate strike since his pilots were so inexperienced in night flying.

Before Ozawa's intentions were clear, the carrier task group closest to TF 58, commanded by the aggressive Rear Admiral Obayashi, did not wait. Thinking that an immediate attack would catch the Americans by surprise in a dusk attack, Obayashi ordered a launch of 67 aircraft from carriers *Zuiho*, *Chitose*, and *Chiyoda* at 1637hrs. The launch was already in progress with 22 aircraft airborne when Ozawa's Operation Order No. 16 issued at 1610hrs arrived. Reluctantly, Obayashi aborted his strike.

Ozawa did a good job assessing Spruance's intentions. Three USN carrier groups had been detected west of Saipan meaning that Ozawa could dismiss his fears of an American threat from the north. He assessed, correctly, that TF 58 would maintain its position relative to Saipan. This meant that Ozawa could maintain his position without fear of an American attack. With this in mind, Ozawa decided to make June 19 the day of decision. At 1540hrs, he ordered a course change to the southwest to maintain at least 400nm from TF 58.

In accordance with its new orders, the First Mobile Fleet assumed a course to the southwest until 1900hrs when it changed to the southeast at 16 knots. At 2100hrs, his force split. The Van Force (also known as Force C) headed due east, and Forces A and B, with the bulk of the carriers, changed course to the south. At 0300hrs, all three forces headed northeasterly and increased speed to 20 knots. Ozawa's plan had been executed flawlessly. He was in position to launch massive strikes against the unsuspecting Americans in the morning.

At 2020hrs, Ozawa took the step of breaking radio silence for the first time during the operation. The message was needed to coordinate the decisive operation planned for June 19 with Kakuta's land-based air forces. The transmission was picked up by an American direction-finding station and geo-located on a fairly accurate basis. Ozawa could not know that by June 19 the Base Air Force was in no shape for any kind of battle, much less a decisive one. Kakuta consistently kept the true condition of his forces from Ozawa while issuing over-optimistic reports of successes by his aviators. Kakuta ordered the last 19 aircraft on Truk to move to Guam on June 19, bringing the total strength of Japanese aircraft in the Marianas to a mere 50.

Movement and search activity of US and Japanese naval forces, June 18–19

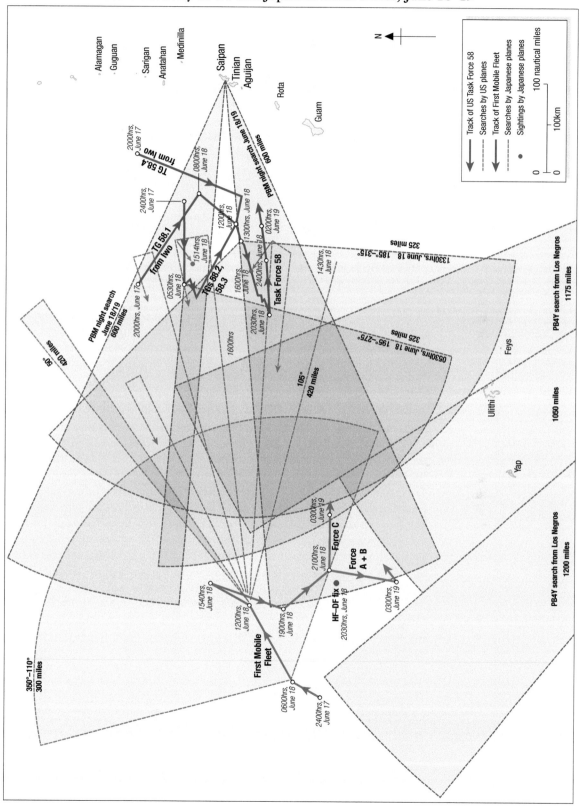

Contrails mark the path of dogfights over TG 58.3 as seen from light cruiser *Birmingham*. This unusual atmospheric condition made interception of Japanese aircraft easier for American fighters. (Naval History and Heritage Command)

THE BATTLE IS JOINED

At noon on the 18th, TGs 58.1 and 58.4 joined, and the entirety of TF 58 headed to the southwest. After advancing 115nm, TF 58 turned to the west at 2030hrs in accordance with Spruance's overall orders to remain near Saipan.

As the largest carrier battle in history brewed, it would be fought under ideal weather conditions. The wind continued to come from the east, favoring the Japanese. Ceiling and visibility were unlimited. Air temperature was in the mid-80s. The clear conditions and the unusual creation of vapor trails by low-flying aircraft were favorable to the Americans; during the battle some Japanese aircraft were spotted by American aviators at distances of up to 35 miles.

Task Force 58 maintained its course to the east until 0530hrs when it turned to the northeast to launch its dawn CAP, search and antisubmarine patrols. Once completed, TF 58 changed course to the west at 0619hrs. Since the American carriers had to return to an easterly heading every time they launched or recovered aircraft, TF 58 drifted to the east throughout the day.

Spruance's battle dispositions were as follows: TGs 58.1, 58.3 and 58.2 were arranged in a line, north to south. The center of each task group was 12–15nm from the next. The battle line, TG 58.7, was deployed 15nm to the west of TG 58.3. Finally, TG 58.4 was to the north of the battle line. For each of the carrier task groups, the carriers were deployed in the center of a circular formation some 4nm in diameter.

The first phase of the battle involved a series of small encounters with Japanese aircraft from the Marianas. Beginning at 0530hrs, Hellcats encountered Japanese aircraft from Guam. On two occasions, Japanese dive-bombers attacked destroyers of TG 58.7, but inflicted no damage.

At 0630hrs, American radar detected Japanese air activity over Guam and four Hellcats were sent to investigate. At 0720hrs, these arrived and found themselves in the middle of many Japanese aircraft taking off. More Hellcats rushed in and, beginning at 0807hrs for the next hour, there was constant combat over and near Guam. Up to 33 American fighters were involved, and they claimed 30 fighters and five bombers. This early morning attempt to suppress Guam, ordered by Spruance, successfully disrupted any attempt by Kakuta to support Ozawa's decisive battle. At 1000hrs, all Hellcats returned to their carriers when American radar detected large formations to the west.

OZAWA ATTACKS

Following the skirmishing over the Marianas, the next few hours would decide the battle. Ozawa had set himself up for the battle he had long planned to fight, and Spruance was prepared to fight the battle he had convinced himself he had to fight. Neither side foresaw the outcome of the actual event.

Tactical disposition of TF 58, June 19

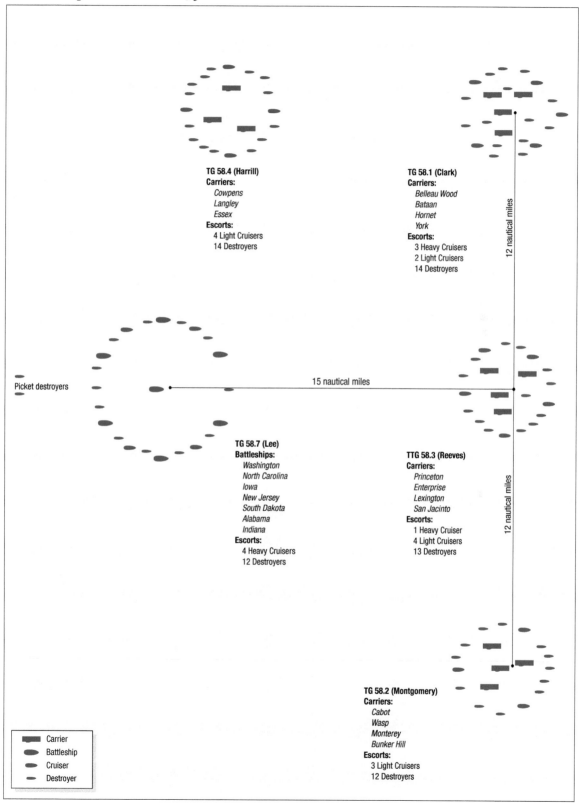

TG 58.4 (Harrill)
Carriers:
Cowpens
Langley
Essex
Escorts:
4 Light Cruisers
14 Destroyers

TG 58.1 (Clark)
Carriers:
Belleau Wood
Bataan
Hornet
York
Escorts:
3 Heavy Cruisers
2 Light Cruisers
14 Destroyers

12 nautical miles

Picket destroyers

15 nautical miles

TG 58.7 (Lee)
Battleships:
Washington
North Carolina
Iowa
New Jersey
South Dakota
Alabama
Indiana
Escorts:
4 Heavy Cruisers
12 Destroyers

TTG 58.3 (Reeves)
Carriers:
Princeton
Enterprise
Lexington
San Jacinto
Escorts:
1 Heavy Cruiser
4 Light Cruisers
13 Destroyers

12 nautical miles

TG 58.2 (Montgomery)
Carriers:
Cabot
Wasp
Monterey
Bunker Hill
Escorts:
3 Light Cruisers
12 Destroyers

Carrier
Battleship
Cruiser
Destroyer

At 0445hrs, the Japanese started to launch their search aircraft. The number devoted to searches was considerable, in keeping with Ozawa's imperative to track the USN's carrier force so he could stay out of its range and by the hard-learned lesson that in carrier battles the side that found the other first had an immense tactical advantage. The first group of search aircraft was comprised of 16 Aichi E13A (Allied reporting name "Jake") floatplanes from the heavy cruisers and battleships of the Van Force. These three-seater floatplanes were vulnerable to interception if detected, but their range of over 1,100nm made them good scouting platforms. By 0700hrs, these aircraft reached the end of their search leg and headed back. On their return track, one of the Jakes spotted the northern elements of TF 58 – the battleships of TG 58.7 and TG 58.4. This detection was designated "7 I" by the Japanese. The second Japanese search, launched at 0515hrs, was conducted by 13 Kates and one Jake from the Van Force. The only thing they sighted was the picket destroyers deployed in front of TG 58.7. For this, seven of the scouts were shot down, several being claimed by Hellcats from light carrier *Langley* of TG 58.4.

OZAWA'S FIRST STRIKE

The detection of the carriers of TG 58.4 was good enough for Ozawa to start launching his strikes. The first strike was launched from the three light carriers of the Van Force and comprised 69 aircraft – 16 Zero fighters, 45 Zeros with bombs and eight Jills with torpedoes. The launch began at 0830hrs some 300 miles from TF 58. The radar from TG 58.7 picked up the raid while still 125nm distant. This gave Mitscher plenty of time to orchestrate a strong interception. At 1023hrs, launching of every available Hellcat from TF 58

A Hellcat from VF-1 on *Yorktown* prepares to take off on June 19. VF-1 made 30 sorties on this day and claimed 32 destroyed Japanese aircraft and five probables. (Naval History and Heritage Command)

Movement and search activity of US and Japanese forces, June 19

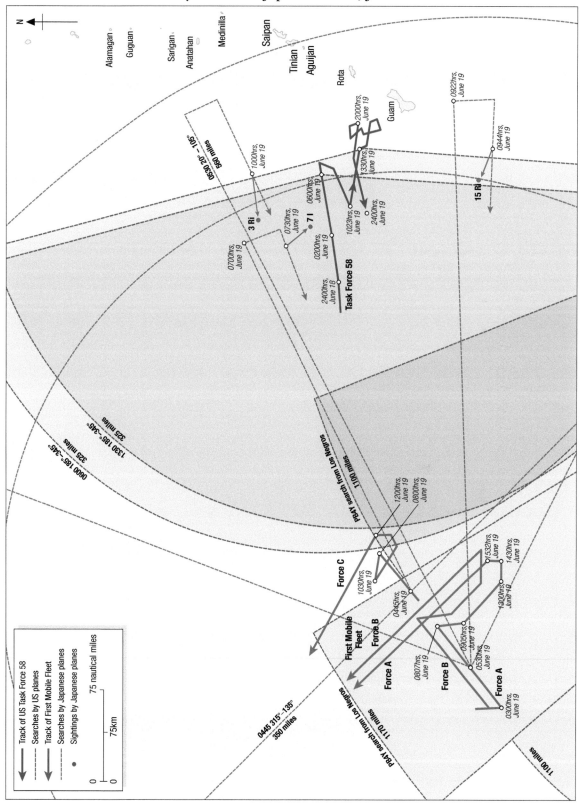

THE AIR BATTLE OF JUNE 19. AMERICAN HELLCAT FIGHTERS WADE INTO THE JAPANESE AIRCRAFT OF RAID I. (PP. 60–61)

The first of the great series of air battles on June 19 began poorly for the Japanese. Use of radar allowed American fighters to intercept the incoming Japanese 55nm from TF 58. The Japanese had no idea the Americans were capable of conducting interceptions this far from their carriers. The first American fighters to sight the Japanese were Hellcats (1) from VF-15 flying off *Essex*. The squadron commander, Commander Charles Brewer, led the Hellcats. He identified the attackers as Judys escorted by Zeros. This was incorrect since there were no Judys present; the strike aircraft were a mix of a small number of Jills (2) and many more Zero fighter-bombers (3). The Japanese formation was divided into two main groups with no apparent breakout into divisions or sections. Behind the Japanese aircraft flying at 18,000ft were thick contrails. The Hellcats dove from 24,000ft to slash through the Japanese

formation. Brewer and his wingman quickly flamed four aircraft each (4). Lieutenant Junior Grade George Carr did even better, claiming five Japanese aircraft in minutes. During this engagement, VF-15 claimed 20 kills. Fighter-direction officers reinforced VF-15 with fighters from *Bunker Hill* and *Hornet*, supported by Hellcats from five light carriers, to finish the destruction of Raid I. After the devastation rendered by the Hellcats, the few remaining Japanese aircraft decided to attack the battleships of TG 58.7. The result was a near-perfect example of fleet air defense. Of the 69 Japanese aircraft, 42 were destroyed, the great majority in air-to-air combat. None of the Japanese pilots spotted, much less attacked, an American carrier. The Japanese pilots proved to be brave, but were over matched by the better-trained American pilots who had the additional advantage of flying better machines.

began as the force headed east into the wind. The American carriers cleared their decks and all airborne bombers on search and patrol missions were instructed to clear the area. This allowed the fighters to return as necessary to rearm and refuel. The goal was to keep as many fighters in the air as possible to intercept incoming threats.

The aircrew of the Van Force's three light carriers were not well trained and this was quickly demonstrated as the strike, designated Raid I by the Americans, approached TF 58. Instead of heading in for their attack, the Japanese orbited at 20,000ft after they had closed to within 70 miles of the American carriers. This gave Mitscher more time to finish launching his fighters and gave the intercepting fighters more time to get to their desired altitudes. The Hellcats had reached their interception altitudes of between 17,000 and 23,000ft when at 1035hrs they spotted the incoming Japanese aircraft identified as two groups of strike aircraft with escorting Zeros on each flank. The first American fighters on the scene were Hellcats from *Essex*. Lieutenant Commander C. Brewer of Fighter Squadron 15 (VF-15) led them. The aggressive Hellcats pummeled the inexperienced Japanese. The escorting Japanese fighters did not protect the bombers and the bombers scattered making them easy to pick off. Brewer claimed four aircraft, and his wingman claimed another four. In all, VF-15 pilots claimed 20 Japanese aircraft. Joining the Hellcats from *Essex* were others from *Hornet* and *Bunker Hill* as well as from five light carriers for a total of 50 Hellcats. Altogether, some 25 out of the 69 Japanese aircraft in this raid were accounted for by this initial interception. In return, three Hellcats were lost in combat and a *Bunker Hill* Hellcat was lost when it ditched on its way back to its carrier.

The remaining Japanese aircraft, some 40 in number, continued inbound. Before reaching their targets, more *Bunker Hill* Hellcats from VF-8 made an interception and claimed another 16. The few remaining Japanese aircraft

Plane handlers aboard *Lexington* rest on the flight deck during a break in the action on June 19. The aircraft in the background are Hellcats of VF-16. This squadron flew 38 sorties during the day and claimed 26 Japanese aircraft destroyed. One Hellcat was lost to operational causes. (Naval History and Heritage Command)

reached the area of TG 58.7 and began a series of small-scale attacks. Two came after battleship *South Dakota*, with one scoring a direct bomb hit at 1049hrs. It killed 27 men and wounded 23, but the damage was light and the ability of the battleship to steam and fight was unimpeded. Another scored a near miss on heavy cruiser *Minneapolis*, and a second near-missed heavy cruiser *Wichita*. Two picket destroyers deployed to the west of the battleships reported coming under attack from a few aircraft, but received no damage.

The results of the first Japanese strike were meager. No USN carrier was even attacked, and only a single bomb hit was gained on an American ship. In return, the Japanese admitted to losing 42 aircraft – eight fighters, 32 fighter-bombers, and two torpedo bombers. Most had been destroyed by Hellcats, with antiaircraft gunnery from TG 58.7 accounting for the rest.

OZAWA'S SECOND STRIKE

BELOW LEFT
Fighter aircraft of TG 58.2 produce condensation trails flying CAP above a carrier before a Japanese air attack on June 19. (Naval History and Heritage Command)

BELOW RIGHT
A Japanese bomber from Raid II scores a near miss on carrier *Bunker Hill*. The bomb killed three, wounded 73, damaged the port-side elevator, started several small fires, blew a Hellcat overboard, and damaged the hangar deck fuel system. The aircraft responsible is to the left, without its tail, headed into the water. (Naval History and Heritage Command)

Ozawa's main punch was up next. This was a large strike (designated Raid II) from the three fleet carriers of Carrier Division 1 with the best-trained aviators in the First Mobile Fleet. The raid consisted of 128 aircraft – 48 Zero fighters, 53 Judy dive-bombers and 27 Jills with torpedoes. Launching began at 0856hrs but was disrupted when at 0909hrs *Taiho* came under attack by American submarine *Albacore*. The submarine fired six torpedoes at the fast-moving carrier. One of *Taiho*'s aircraft saw the torpedoes headed for the ship and dove into one in an effort to save the ship. In spite of this, one of the torpedoes hit the carrier abreast the forward elevator and created a hole which resulting in flooding. The ship's forward elevator, which was raised for the launch, was knocked out of alignment and fell several feet. Within 30 minutes, the elevator space was planked over by damage-control personnel and the launch continued. In addition to the aircraft lost from *Taiho*, eight other aircraft developed engine trouble and were forced to return. More trouble soon followed. When the attack group flew over the Van Force deployed about 100nm in front of the main carrier force, it was engaged by the Japanese ships. This fire was effective enough to shoot down two more aircraft and damage another eight that were forced to return. This left 109 aircraft to deliver the largest Japanese attack of the day.

A Japanese bomb explodes close alongside carrier *Bunker Hill* but this one was too far away to do any damage. (Naval History and Heritage Command)

Approaching TF 58, this group was detected at 1107hrs on radar at least 115nm out which allowed adequate time for another successful interception. The first to arrive was 12 Hellcats from *Essex* led by the ship's air group commander Commander David McCampbell. In a swirling action that began at 1139hrs, the Hellcats again tore through the Japanese formation. McCampbell claimed three Judys and his wingman two. Other Hellcats joined the fray resulting in about 70 Japanese aircraft being shot down. VF-16 from *Lexington* claimed 22 Japanese aircraft without a loss; 12 *Bunker Hill* Hellcats were unable to gain a solid intercept but still claimed

A Japanese aircraft on fire during the noon attack on TG 58.2 in this photo taken from light carrier *Monterey*. (Naval History and Heritage Command)

five kills, and Hellcats from light carriers *Bataan*, *Monterey* and *Cabot* claimed ten, seven and five, respectively. VF-1 from *Yorktown* also scored heavily.

This still left a number of Japanese aircraft headed for TF 58. Twenty were reported in three groups at 1145hrs. Most of these made the mistake of attacking the picket destroyers deployed in advance of TG 58.7 or Lee's battleship force itself. Destroyer *Stockham* reported being under attack for 20 minutes, but again the ship suffered no damage. Around noon, TG 58.7 came under attack. Two torpedo bombers attacked *South Dakota* with no success, and two more

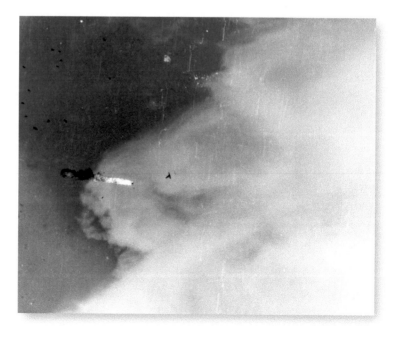

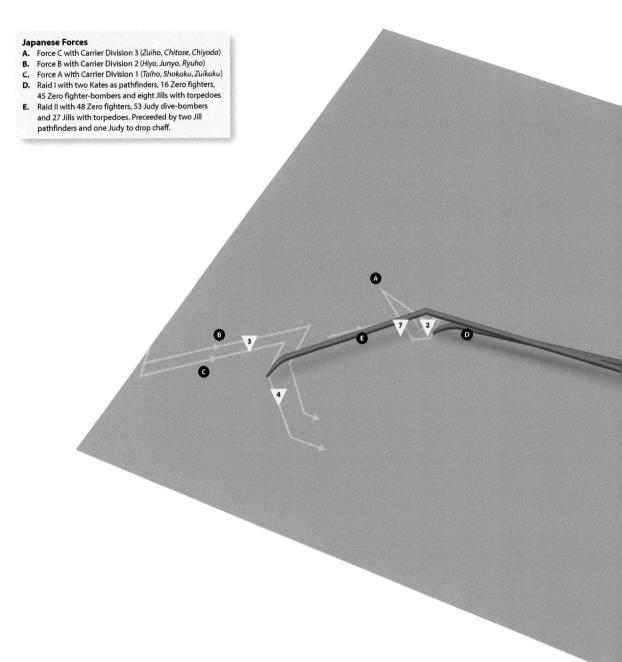

Japanese Forces

A. Force C with Carrier Division 3 (*Zuiho, Chitose, Chiyoda*)
B. Force B with Carrier Division 2 (*Hiyo, Junyo, Ryuho*)
C. Force A with Carrier Division 1 (*Taiho, Shokaku, Zuikaku*)
D. Raid I with two Kates as pathfinders, 16 Zero fighters, 45 Zero fighter-bombers and eight Jills with torpedoes
E. Raid II with 48 Zero fighters, 53 Judy dive-bombers and 27 Jills with torpedoes. Preceeded by two Jill pathfinders and one Judy to drop chaff.

▼ EVENTS

1. 0807hrs: Ozawa receives "7 I" contact report.

2. 0830–0845hrs: Carrier Division 3 launches Raid I.

3. 0856hrs: Carrier Division 1 launches Raid II; eight aircraft return with mechanical damage.

4. 0909hrs: Submarine *Albacore* hits *Taiho* with one torpedo; one *Taiho* aircraft dives into another torpedo.

5. 0945hrs: Japanese search aircraft issue contact "15 Ri."

6. 1000hrs: Japanese search aircraft issue contact "3 Ri."

7. 1000hrs: Raid II flies over Force C; two aircraft shot down and eight forced to return with damage.

8. 1000hrs: battleship *Alabama* detects Raid I at 125 miles.

9. 1023–1037hrs: TF 58 launches additional Hellcats – 220 now airborne.

10. 1035hrs: VF-15 from *Essex* gains contact at 55 miles from TG 58.4 on Raid I. The Hellcats shoot down 25, but about 40 Japanese aircraft get through.

11. 1047hrs: second interception by 12 Hellcats; only scattered Japanese aircraft remain.

12. 1049hrs: Japanese aircraft attack TG 58.7, score hit on *South Dakota* and near misses on two heavy cruisers.

13. 1107hrs: Raid II detected on radar at 115nm west of TG 58.1.

14. 1139hrs: 12 *Essex* F6F Hellcats intercept Raid II at 60 miles from TG 58.4, within minutes are joined by 14 Hellcats from *Cowpens* and fighters from three other carriers.

15. 1159hrs: 16 *Yorktown* fighters intercept ten torpedo aircraft; six Jills attack four battleships but the only damage occurs when one flies into the waterline of *Indiana*.

16. Approximately 1200hrs: six Judy dive-bombers attack TG 58.2; two near misses result in minor damage to *Bunker Hill* and *Wasp*.

17. 1157–1207hrs: six torpedo aircraft attack TG 58.3, but are unsuccessful.

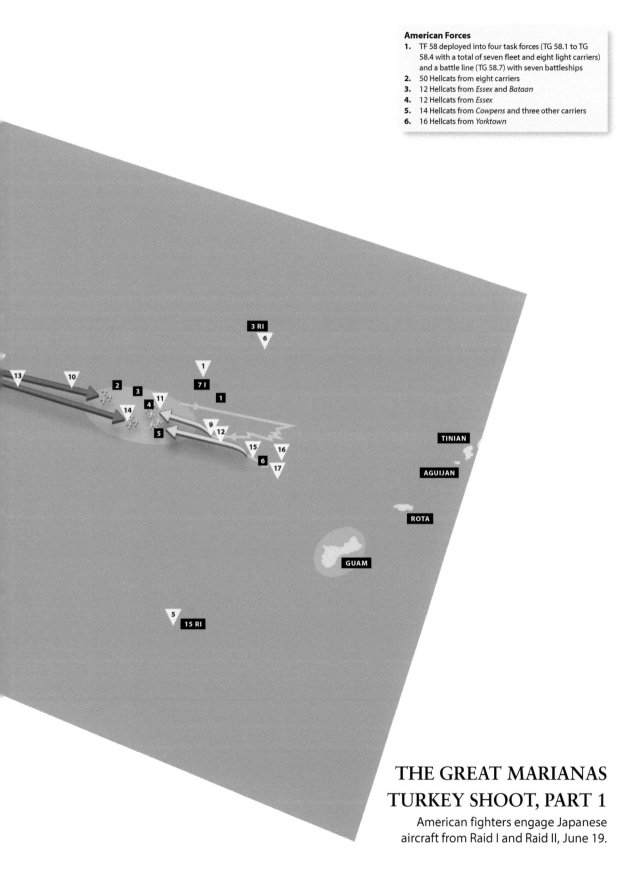

American Forces
1. TF 58 deployed into four task forces (TG 58.1 to TG 58.4 with a total of seven fleet and eight light carriers) and a battle line (TG 58.7) with seven battleships
2. 50 Hellcats from eight carriers
3. 12 Hellcats from *Essex* and *Bataan*
4. 12 Hellcats from *Essex*
5. 14 Hellcats from *Cowpens* and three other carriers
6. 16 Hellcats from *Yorktown*

THE GREAT MARIANAS TURKEY SHOOT, PART 1
American fighters engage Japanese aircraft from Raid I and Raid II, June 19.

selected *Indiana* in the center of TG 58.7's formation as their target. One crashed into the waterline of the heavily armored ship but caused little damage. Another Jill went after *Iowa*, but again missed. *Alabama* was undamaged by two bombs aimed at her.

Potentially more serious was a group of six Judy dive-bombers that escaped the Hellcats and proceeded south until running across TG 58.2. Of this group, four selected carrier *Wasp* for attack. None scored a hit, but one of the bombs detonated overhead which rained down shrapnel that killed one and wounded 12 crewmen. The other two selected TG 58.2's other fleet carrier, *Bunker Hill*, for attack at 1203hrs. They scored two near misses that caused minor fires and other damage, in addition to killing three and wounding 73. Both carriers continued in action. Four of the aircraft were shot down by antiaircraft fire, with the other two landing on Rota and Guam.

The last attack from Raid II was conducted against TG 58.3. This was the work of a small group of six Jills. Again, the Japanese pilots were unable to secure a hit in a series of attacks that began at 1157hrs. One missed *Enterprise*, and another three attacked light carrier *Princeton*, but all three were destroyed by antiaircraft fire.

Ozawa's second strike turned out to be a devastating defeat for the Japanese with 97 of the 128 aircraft never returning to their carriers. Losses included 32 fighter, 42 dive-bombers and 23 Jills. However, these aircraft did have a chance to inflict some damage on TF 58, but the few aircraft that evaded the CAP were unable to deliver their weapons accurately. Even a well-deployed CAP could not hope to destroy all aircraft of a raid this size. Some 20–30 Japanese aircraft survived to conduct attacks on various American ships, but of these only ten exercised discipline in their target selection. The Americans were lucky to have suffered only light damage since none of the enemy aircraft were skillful enough to score a direct hit.

OZAWA'S THIRD STRIKE

Faulty scouting reports from Japanese reconnaissance aircraft impacted Ozawa's remaining two strikes of the day. At 0530hrs, the third group of Japanese scout aircraft took off. This comprised 11 Judys from *Shokaku* and two Jakes from heavy cruiser *Mogami*. The aircraft flew 560nm to the east. Two contacts were radioed back to Ozawa. The first, at 0945hrs, was reported at a position well to the south of TF 58's actual position. The problem resulted from an uncorrected compass deviation on the search aircraft. This contact was designated "15 Ri" by the Japanese. The second contact, designated "3 Ri", was reported at 1000hrs. It was of a task force of three carriers and escorts to the north of TF 58's actual position, but may have been of TG 58.4.

The third Japanese strike (designated Raid III by the Americans) was mounted by Carrier Division 2. This effort, from *Junyo*, *Hiyo* and *Ryuho*, comprised 47 aircraft including 15 fighters, 25 Zeros with bombs, and seven Jills with torpedoes. These took off beginning at 1000hrs and were ordered to attack the old "7 I" contact. After take-off, the attack group was ordered to attack the "3 Ri" contact, but this was not received by most of the aircraft. Twenty-seven aircraft adhered to their original orders and

ABOVE LEFT
A Japanese aircraft from Raid II is shot down attacking TG 58.3. The carrier in the foreground is *Enterprise* and the light carrier in the background either *San Jacinto* or *Princeton*. Note the large bursts from 5in./38 shells and the smaller 40mm bursts. (Naval History and Heritage Command)

ABOVE RIGHT
Several Jill torpedo aircraft from Raid II broke through the CAP to attack TG 58.3. This photo shows antiaircraft fire from *Enterprise* as she engages the incoming Japanese aircraft. The small splash at the center of the intense fire marks the crash of one of the Jills. The carrier at right is either *Princeton* or *San Jacinto*. (Naval History and Heritage Command)

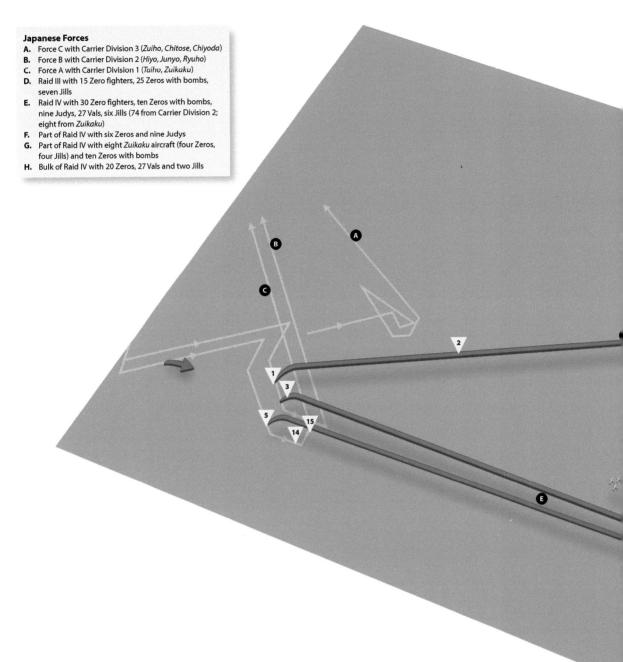

Japanese Forces

A. Force C with Carrier Division 3 (*Zuiho, Chitose, Chiyoda*)
B. Force B with Carrier Division 2 (*Hiyo, Junyo, Ryuho*)
C. Force A with Carrier Division 1 (*Taiho, Zuikaku*)
D. Raid III with 15 Zero fighters, 25 Zeros with bombs, seven Jills
E. Raid IV with 30 Zero fighters, ten Zeros with bombs, nine Judys, 27 Vals, six Jills (74 from Carrier Division 2; eight from *Zuikaku*)
F. Part of Raid IV with six Zeros and nine Judys
G. Part of Raid IV with eight *Zuikaku* aircraft (four Zeros, four Jills) and ten Zeros with bombs
H. Bulk of Raid IV with 20 Zeros, 27 Vals and two Jills

EVENTS

1. 1000hrs: Carrier Division 2 launches Raid III – 15 Zero fighters, seven Jills at contact "7 I."

2. 1030hrs: Raid III ordered to strike "3 Ri."

3. 1100–1130hrs: Raid IV launched from *Zuikaku* and three carriers of Carrier Division 2.

4. Approximately 1200–1300hrs: Finding nothing at the location of "3 Ri," Raid III begins a search. It is tracked on American radar and closes to within 60nm of TG 58.3. Twenty-eight Hellcats are positioned to intercept if the Japanese close on TF 58.

5. 1222hrs: submarine *Cavalla* torpedoes *Shokaku*; the carrier drops out of formation.

6. 1304hrs: eight *Hornet* Hellcats intercept and claim 15 Zeros from Raid III; actual losses are seven aircraft.

7. 1320hrs: a few aircraft from Raid III attack TG 58.4; one drops a bomb 600 yards from *Essex*.

8. Raid IV arrives at location of "15 Ri" and finds nothing. It begins a search before lack of fuel forces most aircraft to head to Guam and Rota. A third group heads back to its carriers.

9. 1421hrs: twelve *Monterey* fighters intercept a group of six Zero fighters and nine Judy dive-bombers within visual range of TG 58.2.

10. 1423hrs: *Bunker Hill* and *Wasp* attacked by dive-bombers.

11. 1443hrs: bulk of Raid IV (20 Zero fighters, 27 Vals, two Jills) detected on radar near Guam.

12. 1449hrs: 27 Hellcats from three carriers intercept the 49 Japanese aircraft landing at Orote Field on Guam; 30 are shot down and the remainder crash land and never fly again.

13. 1500–1530hrs: third group of 18 Japanese aircraft returning to their carriers clashes with two groups of American aircraft and lose six aircraft.

14. 1501hrs: *Shokaku* sinks.

15. 1352hrs: *Taiho* racked by major explosion and later sinks.

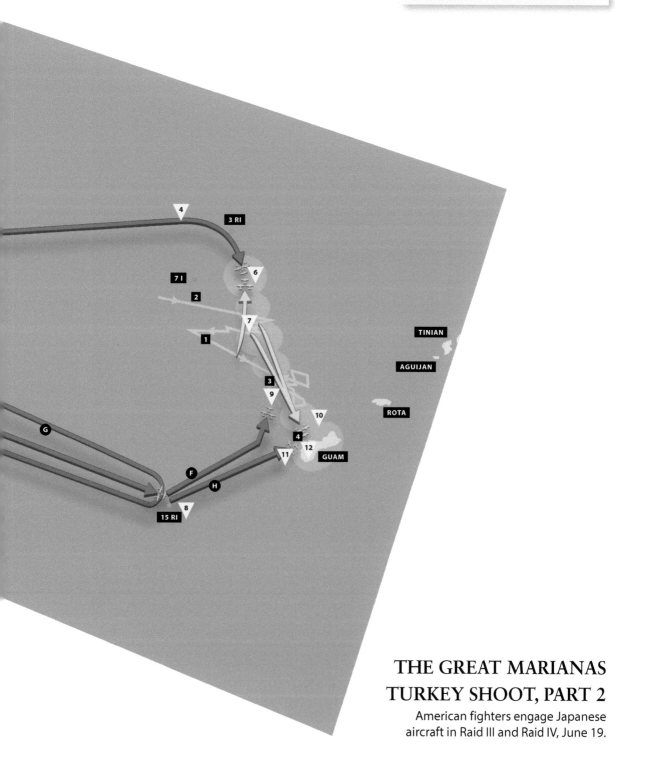

American Forces
1. TF 58 deployed into four task forces (TG 58.1 to TG 58.4 with a total of seven fleet and eight light carriers) and a battle line (TG 58.7) with seven battleships
2. Eight *Hornet* Hellcats
3. 12 *Monterey* Hellcats
4. 27 Hellcats (12 *Cowpens*, seven *Essex*, eight *Hornet*)

3 RI

7 I

TINIAN

AGUIJAN

ROTA

GUAM

15 RI

THE GREAT MARIANAS TURKEY SHOOT, PART 2

American fighters engage Japanese aircraft in Raid III and Raid IV, June 19.

flew to the area of the "7 I" contact, but found nothing. Showing little initiative in this decisive battle, they returned to their carriers without loss. The remaining group of about 20 aircraft headed for the newer contact. They spotted what they claimed to be two battleships, but decided to press on to find carriers. This search was unsuccessful, and the group turned to attack the previously spotted battleships at 1255hrs. At this point, Hellcats from *Hornet* and *Yorktown* intercepted the wandering Japanese and claimed 14 Japanese aircraft destroyed; the actual count was seven aircraft destroyed. At 1320hrs, a few aircraft broke through to attack TG 58.4. The effort was ineffective with one aircraft dropping a bomb 600 yards from *Essex*. The third Japanese strike had accomplished nothing, but at least 40 of its 47 aircraft survived to return to their carriers.

OZAWA'S FOURTH STRIKE

Ozawa's final attack of the day was launched beginning at 1100hrs. This came from Carrier Division 2 and *Zuikaku* from Carrier Division 1. It comprised 30 Zero fighters, ten Zeros with bombs, 36 dive-bombers (27 Vals and nine Judys) and six Jills. *Zuikaku*'s contribution was four Zeros and four Jills. The story of these 82 aircraft is complicated since they were directed at the non-existent "15 Ri" contact and, after finding nothing, split into three smaller groups. The largest group of 20 Zeros, 27 Vals and two Jills headed for Guam. Approaching Guam, they were picked up by TF 58 radar at 1449hrs. Before long, 27 Hellcats were on the scene. Among these were 12 from light carrier *Cowpens*, seven from *Essex* again led by McCampbell, and eight from *Hornet*. The Hellcats did great execution, shooting down 30 of the 49 Japanese trying to land on Guam. The remaining 19 did land, but were damaged and would not fly again.

Another 15 aircraft, probably including six Zeros and nine Judys, headed for Rota but sighted TG 58.2 en route. They changed course to attack, but were detected on radar some 45 miles from the American carriers. The bulk of these got through the CAP which did not make an interception until the Japanese were in visual range of TG 58.2, probably due to the confusion resulting from TG 58.2 being in the process of recovering aircraft. Six aircraft approached *Wasp* unmolested until 1423hrs when they were engaged by antiaircraft fire just as they were dropping their bombs. Adept maneuvering by *Wasp* thwarted the aircraft, identified as Judys. Another group of dive-bombers appeared and split up; two went after *Bunker Hill*, and one after *Wasp*. All missed, and of the nine attackers, only one escaped. The final 18 aircraft of Raid IV, including the eight from *Zuikaku* and ten Zeros with bombs, were returning to their carriers when they encountered two American scout groups consisting of Hellcats and Avengers some 200nm west of Guam. This encounter cost the Japanese six aircraft, but they did gain a measure of revenge when at 1530hrs the same group of returning Japanese aircraft encountered and shot down two *Bunker Hill* aircraft on a search mission.

The final tally for Ozawa's fourth strike was dismal. Of the 82 aircraft, only nine returned to their carriers. Despite these heavy losses, no American ships were hit. Fortune presented the Japanese with another chance to knock an American carrier out of the battle, but this was wasted due to the Japanese pilots' lack of bombing proficiency.

ACTION OVER GUAM

As Ozawa sent his series of strikes against TF 58, Spruance directed Mitscher to keep a number of Hellcats active over Guam to disrupt any Japanese attempt to mount attacks from there. This reflected Spruance's fear that the Japanese would use Guam as a base for "shuttle bombing" using aircraft from the First Mobile Fleet. Before the first Japanese carrier raid, Hellcats encountered airborne Japanese aircraft over Guam. This action continued throughout the day and periodically intensified when TF 58 dive-bombers and Avengers, ordered to the east to steer clear of the air battle, dumped their ordnance on Guam. Before noon, 15 *Yorktown* and 17 *Hornet* Helldivers bombed Orote Field on Guam. Another attack was mounted at 1330hrs by Dauntlesses from *Lexington* and *Enterprise*, nine Avengers from *Enterprise* and ten Hellcats for escort. The armor-piercing bombs carried by the dive-bombers did little damage, but the Avengers succeeded in cratering the runway. Other attacks continued throughout the afternoon including Hellcats from *Bunker Hill* strafing Japanese aircraft on the ground and 11 Helldivers from *Essex* just before 1400hrs.

Lieutenant Junior Grade Alexander Vraciu holds up six fingers to indicate his kills on June 19. He was assigned to VF-16 and was one of six TF 58 pilots who claimed five or more kills on June 19 to become an ace in a single day. By the end of the war, he had 19 kills making him the USN's fourth-highest ace. (Naval History and Heritage Command)

This pre-emptive action proved its worth when the bulk of Ozawa's fourth strike showed up to land at 1449hrs. The 19 that survived the Hellcats were wrecked upon landing. The final act of the day took place at 1845hrs when four Hellcats led by Commander Brewer, commander of VF-15 from *Essex*, was jumped by a large number of Zeros. Brewer and two other Hellcats were shot down. The price to keep Guam suppressed during the day was steep – six Hellcats and one Helldiver – but the Base Air Force did not support Ozawa's main attack.

USN SUBMARINES VERSUS THE FIRST MOBILE FLEET

After *Cavalla*'s report of Ozawa's force at 0730hrs on June 18, Lockwood moved four boats, *Finback*, *Bang*, *Stingray* and *Albacore*, from their positions northwest of Saipan to a new patrol position 250nm to the south. This was an excellent move since it placed these submarines right in the path of the First Mobile Fleet's track. Lockwood gave them orders to shoot first and report later.

Lockwood's placement paid off handsomely on the 19th. *Albacore* found herself right in the middle of Ozawa's Carrier Division 1 with its sparse antisubmarine screen of seven destroyers. *Albacore*'s skipper began tracking a carrier at 0816hrs, and by 0909hrs, he was in a position to fire a full spread at *Taiho*. A last-second glitch in the boat's fire-control computer made it necessary to fire the six torpedoes by eye. One hit, and another may have but for the self-sacrificing action by one of *Taiho*'s aircraft which had just taken off. The single torpedo that hit struck on the forward side

THE TORPEDOING OF JAPANESE AIRCRAFT CARRIER *SHOKAKU*, JUNE 19, BY SUBMARINE *CAVALLA*. (PP. 74–75)

Submarine *Cavalla*, under the command of Lieutenant Commander H. J. Kossler, had been trying to regain contact on the First Mobile Fleet since it lost contact on June 17. Kossler's persistence paid off when at 1152hrs on June 19 he raised his periscope to find himself in the middle of Force A. He spotted *Shokaku* **(1)** recovering aircraft. Kossler began an approach, raising his periscope three more times. The Japanese destroyer *Urakaze* **(2)** was steaming on the starboard beam of the carrier but never detected the presence of the American submarine. When he had closed to 1,000 yards, Kossler fired six torpedoes and went deep **(3)**. Three of the torpedoes hit on the starboard side; two forward and a third amidships **(4)**. Belatedly, *Urakaze* turned to attack *Cavalla*, but it was too late. Kossler counted 106 depth charges, half fairly close, but he and his boat survived to tell of his exploits in sinking the largest ship by an American submarine thus far in the war. Three torpedoes overwhelmed *Shokaku*'s capacity to take damage. Large fuel fires began in the hangar and the ship took a list to starboard. Counterflooding to port overcompensated, creating a port list. As the hangar deck fire grew worse, the doomed carrier came to a halt. The ship began to settle by the bow due to flooding forward. The fires could not be controlled and induced large fuel-fed explosions. Just before 1500hrs, the ship's captain ordered the crew to "Abandon Ship." Before the crew could get off, *Shokaku*'s bow dipped under causing the ship to sink bow first. This sudden development caused a heavy loss of life – 1,272 men.

abreast the forward elevator. It jammed the elevator, but more importantly cracked the forward aviation fuel tank. Soon a mix of water and fuel oil filled the well of the forward elevator. Since the ship continued on at 26 knots, and there were no fires, the new carrier appeared to be only slightly wounded. However, this single hit on the IJN's newest and best-protected carrier was fatal. Damage-control personnel turned on fans throughout the ship to ventilate the fumes from the aviation fuel and the volatile Tarakan crude oil used for fuel. Instead of ventilating the fumes, it spread them throughout the ship which made *Taiho* a floating bomb. At 1532hrs, the inevitable occurred when a massive explosion rocked *Taiho*, heaving up her flight deck and blowing holes in her hull that caused the ship to begin settling. A destroyer took off Ozawa and his staff, but 660 of her crew were lost when she settled on an even keel by the bow.

More disaster was to befall the First Mobile Fleet at the hands of American submarines. Some 60nm away from where *Taiho* was struck, *Cavalla* sighted *Shokaku* recovering aircraft at 1152hrs. *Cavalla*'s skipper skillfully closed the range to 1,000 yards as an oblivious Japanese destroyer patrolled nearby. *Cavalla* fired a full salvo of six torpedoes, and three hit the carrier's starboard side at 1222hrs. The effect was immediate with fires in the hangar deck and a list to starboard. Soon, the ship came to a halt and was left behind when Carrier Division 1 moved north. At 1310hrs, the fires on the hangar set off a bomb that set off fumes from the cracked forward fuel tank. Large explosions ensued and it was obvious the carrier was doomed. At 1501hrs, the Pearl Harbor veteran suddenly sank bow first, taking down 1,272 of her crew.

THE TALLY FOR JUNE 19

The numbers from the carrier air battle of the 19th were staggering. In their four strikes, the Japanese had launched 373 aircraft; of these 243 were lost. Added to these losses were another 50 from Guam, nine when *Shokaku* went down, and another 13 from *Taiho* to bring the total to 315. Returning American fighter pilots agreed that the caliber of Japanese pilots was low with the fighters displaying ignorance of sound tactics in favor of executing acrobatic maneuvers and the bomber pilots quick to disperse their formations when under attack, making a coordinated attack impossible.

For the loss of 315 aircraft, the Japanese received a very weak return. Several surface ships had been attacked, but only a single direct hit was recorded, and that on a heavily armored battleships which had little effect. Carriers *Wasp* and *Bunker Hill* received minor damage but remained in action. American aircraft losses were also light in comparison. Some 296 Hellcats had been engaged during the day in combat, and only 14 were lost in combat with another six recorded as operational losses.

A Hellcat from VF-16 recovers aboard *Lexington* on June 19. Of the 403 Hellcat missions flown during the day, 287 reported engaging a total of 548 Japanese aircraft. Thirteen Hellcats were lost to enemy aircraft, one to friendly antiaircraft fire and six to operational causes during the day. (Naval History and Heritage Command)

Movement, search and strike activity of US and Japanese forces, June 20

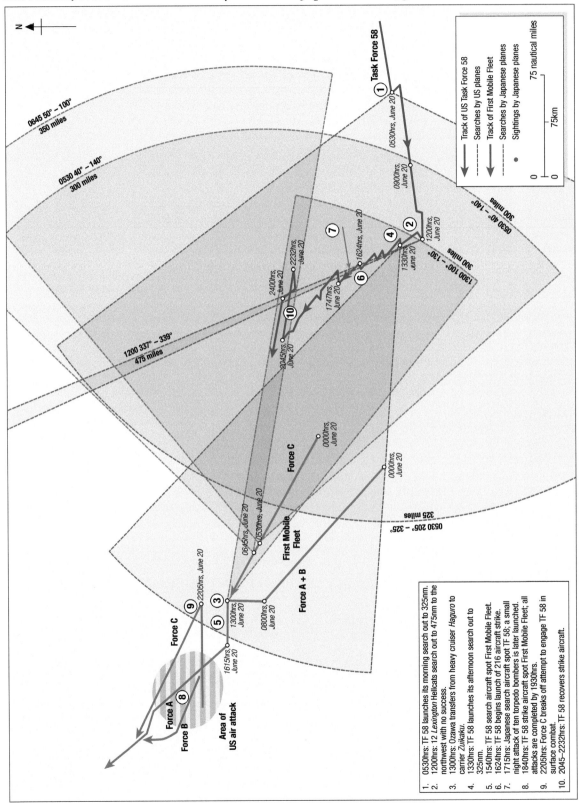

Legend:
- Track of US Task Force 58
- Searches by US planes
- Track of First Mobile Fleet
- Searches by Japanese planes
- Sightings by Japanese planes

0 ———— 75 nautical miles
0 ———— 75km

1. 0530hrs: TF 58 launches its morning search out to 325nm.
2. 1200hrs: 12 *Lexington* Helicats search out to 475nm to the northwest with no success.
3. 1300hrs: Ozawa transfers from heavy cruiser *Haguro* to carrier *Zuikaku*.
4. 1330hrs: TF 58 launches its afternoon search out to 325nm.
5. 1540hrs: TF 58 search aircraft spot First Mobile Fleet.
6. 1624hrs: TF 58 begins launch of 216 aircraft strike.
7. 1715hrs: Japanese search aircraft spot TF 58; a small night attack of ten torpedo bombers is later launched.
8. 1840hrs: TF 58 strike aircraft spot First Mobile Fleet; all attacks are completed by 1930hrs.
9. 2205hrs: Force C breaks off attempt to engage TF 58 in surface combat.
10. 2045–2232hrs: TF 58 recovers strike aircraft.

THE AMERICANS STRIKE BACK

The scope of the disaster on the 19th was not readily apparent to Ozawa. He had no idea of the extent of his aircraft losses. While it was clear that few aircraft had returned to their carriers, he was hopeful that many had recovered at Guam and Rota and were still available for operations. Accordingly, he turned to the northwest at 1808hrs on June 19 and prepared to take fuel on the following day before renewing the attack. This was the basic premise of *A-Go* – a relentless series of attacks to destroy the American carriers. Reports from Japanese aviators gave Ozawa reason to believe that this process was already underway. The returning aviators reported four American carriers sunk and six others left smoking. Adding to the confusion for Ozawa was the fact that he and his staff were jammed into inadequate facilities aboard heavy cruiser *Haguro* after they were forced to depart from *Taiho*. Communications were grossly inadequate; Ozawa admitted later that he should have turned over command to Kurita until he could have moved to a ship with adequate command and control facilities.

The plan to refuel the First Mobile Fleet on June 20 collapsed amidst more confusion. For some three hours from 0920hrs, the two oiler groups and the three carrier task groups milled about without even beginning to refuel until Ozawa canceled the attempt after noon. At 1300hrs, Ozawa and his staff transferred to the fleet carrier *Zuikaku*. At this point, with communications re-established, he learned the true scope of the losses the day before. Japanese records indicate that the First Mobile Fleet was down to 100 aircraft – 32 on *Zuikaku*, 46 on the three carriers of Carrier Division 2 and 22 on Carrier Division 3. Ozawa's hope that he could continue strikes was buoyed by reports from Kakuta that some of Ozawa's aircraft had landed on Guam and the prospects that additional land-based aircraft reinforcements would flow into the area. The only concession he made was to move his next attack until the 21st. Not until 1645hrs did Ozawa give up and head to the northwest at 24 knots following intercepted reports from American aviators at 1615hrs that the First Mobile Fleet had been sighted. This indicated that TF 58 was near, perhaps close enough to launch strikes.

Even in defeat, the Japanese continued to excel at reconnaissance. On June 20, Japanese morning search activity included nine float planes and six carrier aircraft from the Van Force. These encountered only American search aircraft, but this, combined with reports from land-based search aircraft, which reported elements of TF 58, were enough for Kurita to advise an immediate withdrawal. Three carrier aircraft launched in the afternoon found TF 58 at 1715hrs, and Ozawa used this information to launch a night attack from the Force C with seven Kates led by three radar-equipped Jills.

While Ozawa pondered whether and how to resume the battle, Spruance was determined to hit the Japanese carriers on the 20th. For most of the 19th, TF 58 tracked to the east to launch and recover aircraft. By 1500hrs, Mitscher's flagship *Lexington* was only 20 miles off Guam. It was not until 2000hrs, after recovering all aircraft, that TF 58 took a westerly course and increased speed to 23 knots in an effort to close the distance to the First Mobile Fleet. Mitscher detached TG 58.4 to refuel and suppress Japanese air activity on Guam and Rota. The other three carrier groups, led by TG 58.7 by some 25 miles, eagerly looked forward to the chance to engage the Japanese the following day.

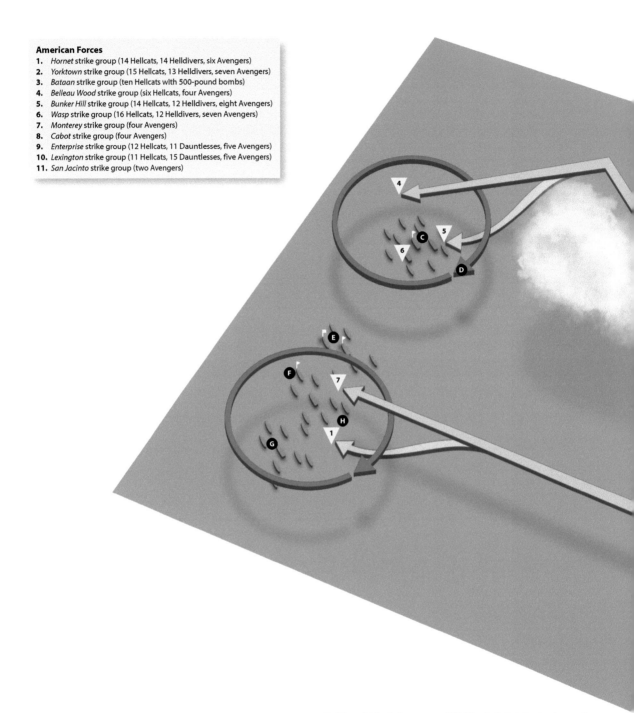

American Forces
1. *Hornet* strike group (14 Hellcats, 14 Helldivers, six Avengers)
2. *Yorktown* strike group (15 Hellcats, 13 Helldivers, seven Avengers)
3. *Bataan* strike group (ten Hellcats with 500-pound bombs)
4. *Belleau Wood* strike group (six Hellcats, four Avengers)
5. *Bunker Hill* strike group (14 Hellcats, 12 Helldivers, eight Avengers)
6. *Wasp* strike group (16 Hellcats, 12 Helldivers, seven Avengers)
7. *Monterey* strike group (four Avengers)
8. *Cabot* strike group (four Avengers)
9. *Enterprise* strike group (12 Hellcats, 11 Dauntlesses, five Avengers)
10. *Lexington* strike group (11 Hellcats, 15 Dauntlesses, five Avengers)
11. *San Jacinto* strike group (two Avengers)

EVENTS

1. 1803hrs: Japanese radar from Force C detects incoming American strike; 40 fighters and 28 fighter-bombers airborne on CAP.

2. *Wasp* strike group attacks Japanese supply group; tankers *Genyo Maru* and *Seiyo Maru* disabled and later scuttled.

3. Strike groups from *Yorktown*, *Hornet* and *Bataan* attack Force A. *Zuikaku*, defended by 17 fighters, avoids the four torpedoes aimed at her and takes a single direct bomb hit. The Americans lose three aircraft to antiaircraft fire. The Japanese lose six fighters.

4. Strike groups from *Lexington*, *Belleau Wood*, *San Jacinto* and *Enterprise*, assisted by Hellcats and Avengers from *Yorktown* and Hellcats from *Hornet* carrying bombs, attack Force B defended by as many as 38 fighters. *Lexington*'s dive-bombers go after *Junyo* and *Hiyo* and score bomb hits against both carriers. *Lexington*'s Avengers also attack *Junyo*. Three aircraft are lost to defending fighters.

5. *Ryuho* is attacked by Avengers from *Enterprise* but suffers only near misses though the Americans claim eight hits. *Ryuho* also escapes damage from *Enterprise*'s dive-bombers and *Yorktown*'s Avengers, five carrying torpedoes.

6. The Avengers from *Belleau Wood* select *Hiyo* for attack; one torpedo hit proves fatal.

7. Force C is attacked by the strike groups from *Bunker Hill*, *Monterey* and *Cabot*. Force C is organized into three groups each centered around a light carrier with several escorting battleships and heavy cruisers for antiaircraft protection. Only the *Chiyoda* group was attacked; the light carrier takes a single direct bomb hit, *Haruna* is struck by a bomb, and *Maya* suffers slight damage from a near miss. Two fighters from *Bunker Hill* are lost.

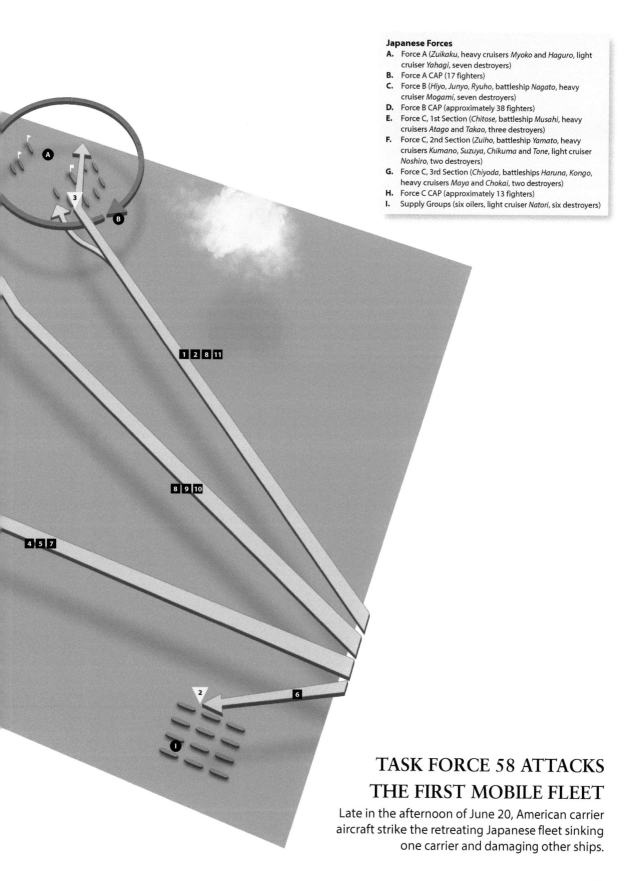

Japanese Forces
A. Force A (*Zuikaku*, heavy cruisers *Myoko* and *Haguro*, light cruiser *Yahagi*, seven destroyers)
B. Force A CAP (17 fighters)
C. Force B (*Hiyo*, *Junyo*, *Ryuho*, battleship *Nagato*, heavy cruiser *Mogami*, seven destroyers)
D. Force B CAP (approximately 38 fighters)
E. Force C, 1st Section (*Chitose*, battleship *Musahi*, heavy cruisers *Atago* and *Takao*, three destroyers)
F. Force C, 2nd Section (*Zuiho*, battleship *Yamato*, heavy cruisers *Kumano*, *Suzuya*, *Chikuma* and *Tone*, light cruiser *Noshiro*, two destroyers)
G. Force C, 3rd Section (*Chiyoda*, battleships *Haruna*, *Kongo*, heavy cruisers *Maya* and *Chokai*, two destroyers)
H. Force C CAP (approximately 13 fighters)
I. Supply Groups (six oilers, light cruiser *Natori*, six destroyers)

TASK FORCE 58 ATTACKS THE FIRST MOBILE FLEET

Late in the afternoon of June 20, American carrier aircraft strike the retreating Japanese fleet sinking one carrier and damaging other ships.

Any hope of engaging the Japanese the next day was dependent on good reconnaissance. This had proven the principal weakness of USN carrier operations in previous battles and would prove so again. Despite the fact that each fleet carrier had a detachment of night fighters capable of conducting searches, these were not used on the night of June 19–20. Throughout the 20th, TF 58 showed little urgency in conducting searches. At 0530hrs, Mitscher launched the usual morning search that went out 325nm. Since the First Mobile Fleet was 75 miles beyond this, the search aircraft found nothing. Around noon Mitscher was convinced to send out a group of 12 Hellcats from *Lexington* flown by volunteers out to 475nm to the northwest, but these also failed to find any sign of Ozawa. The Japanese reverted to radio silence during the day, and no additional information was gained by American submarines in the area or PBM flying boats operating from Saipan. This lack of information on Japanese movements placed Spruance in a difficult situation since the later it got into the afternoon the less likely he could launch a strike without making a risky night recovery.

The afternoon search, launched at 1330hrs, again out to the usual 325nm, finally made contact. At 1540hrs, an *Enterprise* Avenger was the first aviator to spot the First Mobile Fleet during the battle. The aircraft's first report was garbled, but by 1553hrs Mitscher had informed Spruance that he was planning an all-out strike. Spruance let the planned strike continue, even though he knew the risks involved. With the sun setting at 1900hrs, the strike would be recovered after dark. Later spotting reports from the contact aircraft provided a corrected position 60nm further west. This meant that the Japanese fleet was 275 miles from TF 58 – well past maximum strike range. When he learned of the additional range to the target, Mitscher canceled the launch of the second deckload of strike aircraft. While this risky attack represented probably the only chance for TF 58 to get at the Japanese, the net result of a strike launched at this distance and at this time of day was that the aircraft committed would suffer heavy attrition, and even if recovered, would not be available the next day.

TF 58 ATTACKS

The launch began at 1624hrs and took only 12 minutes. Into the air went a full deckload from 11 carriers – 85 Hellcats, 77 dive-bombers (51 Helldivers and 26 Dauntlesses) and 54 Avengers (of which only 12 were armed with torpedoes). After an uneventful flight, they spotted the First Mobile Fleet at 1840hrs. Since they were at the end of their endurance after having flown almost 300 miles, there was no time to launch a coordinated attack. What ensued was a series of individual attacks that was over in about 30 minutes.

The First Mobile Fleet was not well positioned to meet the attack. The Van Force with most of the heavy escorts and the best antiaircraft capabilities was not the closest formation to the incoming American strike. Each of Ozawa's three groups was headed northwesterly with the Van Force

Seen from light cruiser *Birmingham*, a strike group of Hellcats, Dauntlesses and Avengers fly over carrier *Lexington*. The aircraft have just taken off on the afternoon of June 20 and are heading to attack the First Mobile Fleet. *Lexington*'s deck load strike contributed 11 Hellcats, 16 Dauntlesses (one aborted) and six Avengers (armed with bombs, but one aborted after launch). Only *Lexington* and *Enterprise* from TG 58.3 still had Dauntless dive-bombers in their air groups. (Naval History and Heritage Command)

to the south, Carrier Division 2 in the center and *Zuikaku* to the north. Astern of the carrier groups were the two supply groups composed of six oilers with their escorts, making this the closest group to the Americans. At 1803hrs the Japanese detected the American strike on radar which probably gave them sufficient time to launch the 40 fighters and 28 fighter-bombers still available.

The air groups from *Hornet* and *Yorktown* and the ten bomb-carrying Hellcats from *Bataan* selected *Zuikaku* for attack. The veteran carrier was defended by 17 fighters and put up a good fight with heavy antiaircraft fire and adept maneuvering. She avoided the four torpedoes aimed at her from the *Hornet* Avengers and took only a single direct hit by a 500-pound bomb aft of the island. After departing, the Americans reported the big carrier with heavy fires onboard. However, the damage was not as great as it appeared. The single bomb hit penetrated to the upper hanger deck where a fire started among the remaining aircraft. These were not fueled, so

A group of Helldivers and Avengers en route to attack the First Mobile Fleet on the afternoon of June 20. The shorter-ranged Helldivers suffered heavily in the ensuing return to TF 58. Of the 51 that set out to attack, four were lost in combat and 39 lost operationally for a loss rate of 84 percent. (Naval History and Heritage Command)

after a few tense moments and an order to abandon ship that was quickly rescinded, the fire was extinguished. Six near misses were recorded, but overall damage was light. *Zuikaku*, the last surviving carrier from the Pearl Harbor attack force, lived to fight again.

The strike group from *Lexington*, assisted by the Avengers from *Enterprise*, *Yorktown* and *Belleau Wood*, attacked Force B that was defended by as many as 38 fighters. Hellcats from *Hornet* and *Yorktown* carrying 500-pound bombs also rolled in. Most of *Lexington*'s Dauntless dive-bombers selected *Junyo* for attention. At 1904hrs, one or two bombs hit the carrier's island, and several near misses created minor flooding. Casualties included 53 dead, but overall damage was light. Light carrier *Ryuho* was attacked by the five Avengers from *Enterprise* with bombs at 1910hrs; eight hits were claimed, but only slight damage was caused by near misses. The carrier also survived attacks from *Enterprise* Dauntlesses, Avengers from *Yorktown* (five with torpedoes) and probably Hellcats from *Hornet*.

Hiyo suffered the most successful attack of the evening. The carrier left the formation to launch two Jills to lay a smoke screen and was caught behind the main body when the American strike arrived. In the opening attack by Dauntlesses from *Lexington*, one bomb hit the foremast and exploded above the bridge resulting in heavy casualties to bridge personnel. The Japanese reported that another bomb hit the flight deck. However, the group of four *Belleau Wood* Avengers with torpedoes caused fatal damage. Three conducted an anvil attack, and one torpedo hit the carrier's starboard engine room. This was followed by a dive-bomb attack from six *Enterprise* Dauntlesses. The single torpedo hit, the only one scored by Avengers during the entire attack, proved fatal to the largely unprotected carrier. Within minutes, the damage created a list. The ship proceeded for a time on its port engine, but then went dead in the water. Just before sunset, at 1917hrs, there was a large explosion amidships that caused a loss of power. The Japanese were convinced that this was the result of a submarine-launched torpedo,

THE ATTACK ON *HIYO*. (PP. 84–85)

The American air attack on the First Mobile Fleet during the early evening of June 20 was a hurried affair. Only a handful of bombs found their mark during the attack. Only one of the 12 Avengers armed with torpedoes made a successful attack. This success was due to a group of four Avengers from light carrier *Belleau Wood* led by Lt. Junior Grade George Brown **(1)**. Before taking off, Brown swore he would torpedo a carrier whatever the cost. Now was his chance to deliver on that promise. He and his group circled Force B before picking *Hiyo* **(2)** as their target. Placing the sun behind him, Brown dove through a cloud and spread his three remaining aircraft (the fourth was separated in the turn) out to attack from different angles. Brown's Avenger was

hit by 25mm antiaircraft fire that shot off part of the port wing and caused a fire that forced the radiomen and gunner to bail out **(3)**. As Brown's aircraft pressed the attack, the fire onboard burned out. The three Avengers launched their torpedoes from different angles virtually ensuring a hit. One torpedo hit *Hiyo* on her starboard quarter **(4)**, but it remains unclear if the torpedo came from Brown's aircraft or another Avenger flown by Lt. Junior Grade Warren Omark. Though Japanese and American sources differ, it seems more likely that Omark delivered the fatal blow. Brown did not make it back to *Belleau Wood*. The severely wounded pilot, under escort by Omark, flew into a cloud after dark and was never seen again.

The only remaining carrier of Force A came under heavy attack during the late afternoon attack. *Zuikaku* is maneuvering wildly with several near misses from bombs all around her. Two escorting destroyers are also seen. Despite the attention given to her by as many as 50 Avengers and Helldivers, *Zuikaku* suffered only a single bomb hit and survived. (Naval History and Heritage Command)

but there were no submarines in the area. A fuel-fed conflagration ensued, causing multiple explosions. The fire was beyond being contained, and the order to abandon ship was given. At 2032hrs, the carrier sank stern-first taking down 35 officers and 212 enlisted men. It seems likely that the explosion was caused by fuel vapors which made *Hiyo* the third carrier to be lost in this manner during the battle. By the end of day, the two surviving carriers of Carrier Division 2 had only 11 fighters, five fighter-bombers and one Jill.

Aircraft from *Bunker Hill*, *Monterey* and *Cabot* attacked Force C. The Japanese were organized into three groups, each centered on a light carrier with several escorting battleships or heavy cruisers. The *Zuiho* and *Chitose* groups were not attacked, but the *Chiyoda* group was. The light carrier was the target of over 20 Helldivers and Avengers with bombs, but only a single bomb hit *Chiyoda* on the flight deck resulting in 20 dead, 30 wounded and two aircraft destroyed. The Avengers from *Monterey* probably scored the single hit, which caused a fire that was quickly extinguished. *Chiyoda* successfully dodged five torpedoes from *Bunker Hill* Avengers and lived to fight another day. Escorting battleship *Haruna* was hit by a 500-pound bomb that penetrated her stern and flooded the steering compartment. The ship's speed was reduced, and 15 crewmen were killed and 19 wounded. Heavy cruiser *Maya* received a near miss from a bomb that caused flooding.

The aircraft from *Wasp*, running low on fuel, decided to attack Ozawa's Supply Group with the idea that the destruction of the oilers would impede the withdrawal of the First Mobile Fleet. *Genyo Maru* and *Seiyo Maru* were damaged by

Bunker Hill's contribution to the June 20 strike was eight Hellcats, 12 Helldivers and eight Avengers with bombs. This photo from a *Bunker Hill* aircraft shows their attack on Force C. The ship in the lower part of the photo is battleship *Haruna* or *Kongo*, both of which were assigned to escort light carrier *Chiyoda*. The primary target was the light carrier *Chiyoda*, seen on the upper right, which took a single bomb hit but suffered only light damage. (Naval History and Heritage Command)

Another view of Force C under attack taken by an aircraft from *Bunker Hill*. In the lower right is heavy cruiser *Maya* or *Chokai* and in the center right is the light carrier *Chiyoda* surrounded by bomb splashes. Note the small number of antiaircraft burst above the formation – a much different picture from the scene over an American task group under air attack. Note also that the ships are maneuvering independently under attack rather than maintaining a formation to provide protection for the carrier. Moving in a circle was favored by the Japanese as an evasion maneuver since it drastically changed the target aspect for dive-bombers. (Naval History and Heritage Command)

Ships of Force C under attack in this view from an Avenger from light carrier *Monterey*. *Chiyoda* maneuvers in the middle left portion of the photo while two large escorts can be seen to the right. A destroyer maneuvers in the lower center of the photo. Two battleships and two heavy cruisers were assigned to provide antiaircraft protection to the light carrier. Twenty-eight USN strike aircraft attacked the *Chiyoda* group, but only scored one direct hit and a single damaging near miss. (Naval History and Heritage Command)

bombs and later scuttled. Fleet oiler *Hayasui* was hit by a bomb and took two near misses, but the crew put the fire out and the ship survived.

In this series of uncoordinated attacks, the Americans lost 20 aircraft including at least six to antiaircraft fire and 12 to defending fighters. The hurried attacks at dusk in the face of a determined Japanese defense resulted in a disappointing return. The lack of bombing accuracy showed the lack of practice by TF 58 against fast-moving naval targets. Only a single torpedo found its mark. In total, one Japanese carrier was sunk by a torpedo, and another two suffered light damage from bombs. Had more than 12 Avengers been armed with torpedoes, the results could have been greater. Of the 100 aircraft available to the Japanese at noon on the 20th, 65, mostly on defensive CAP, were shot down or lost due to operational reasons during the day. Added to this was the loss of 15 of the 27 remaining floatplanes.

Worse was to come for the Americans in the ensuing night recovery. The distance from the targets to TF 58 was between 240 and 300 miles, so fuel exhaustion was a real danger for many pilots. On a dark night, the returning aircraft began to return to their carriers at 2045hrs. Mitscher decided to ignore the potential Japanese air and submarine threats and ordered his ships to use extra illumination beyond the normal landing lights on each carrier deck to guide his appreciative aviators home. Any pretense of order was quickly lost and soon aircraft were ordered to land on any deck in sight. Almost half of the returning aircraft landed on the wrong carrier. This

hectic scene took over two hours to play out. When the final accounting was complete, aircraft losses were expectedly heavy. In addition to the 20 aircraft lost in combat, another 80 were lost in crashes or by ditching. Aboard the 100 lost aircraft were 100 pilots and 109 aircrewmen. After an extensive effort to rescue these downed fliers lasting several days, only 16 pilots and 33 aircrewmen remained unaccounted for.

Admiral Toyoda ordered Ozawa to break off the decisive battle at 2046hrs. At 2205hrs, Ozawa ordered Kurita to break off his advance to the east in search of night surface combat and change course to the northwest. TF 58 maintained a slow pursuit, more in the hope of catching any Japanese cripples than in any hope of catching and re-engaging Ozawa's fleet. All of Ozawa's ships were able to escape, and information from American scout aircraft early on June 21 placing the First Mobile Fleet 360 miles from TF 58 convinced Spruance that there was little chance of catching Ozawa. Finding no cripples, Spruance ordered the chase abandoned at 2030hrs on June 21. The shattered First Mobile Fleet arrived at Okinawa in the afternoon of June 22, marking the end of the battle.

THE AFTERMATH

The conclusion of the battle meant it was time to take stock and assess the results. To the Japanese, the results were clear. Of their nine carriers, three were sunk and two damaged. The most evident sign of defeat was that, of the 430 carrier aircraft available to Ozawa at the start of the battle, only 35 remained on June 21. Added to these extreme losses were all but 12 of the original 43 floatplanes and an unknown number of aircraft from Guam. Altogether, Japanese aircraft loses on June 19–20 amounted to almost 500. The decisive battle had been fought and lost. The IJN's carrier force was shattered and Saipan would fall by July 10 with mop-up of Japanese stragglers continuing into August. This marked a clear turning point for Japan since defeat in the Marianas meant that the horrors of war would soon be visited on the Home Islands.

For the Americans, the results seemed disappointing. It was clear that Japanese naval air power had been destroyed, but even with an overwhelming advantage, the Japanese fleet had not been destroyed. American intelligence confirmed the loss of the three carriers, but the bulk of the Japanese fleet had escaped. The cost to the USN was comparatively light – 130 aircraft and 76 aviators. None of the ships damaged by Japanese attacks on June 19 were placed out of service.

The battle of the Philippine Sea was a carrier battle unlike any other fought during the war. Instead of seeking to strike first, the clear key to victory in the previous four carrier battles, the Americans fought a defensive battle and banked on being able to parry a massive Japanese first strike. In 1942, this Japanese strike would have been crippling; by 1944 the combination of poor Japanese aircrew training and American radar-directed fighter interception made even a large Japanese strike ineffective. However, as startling as the results of the air battle of June 19 were, the performance of the USN's CAP was not flawless. Several small groups of Japanese aircraft broke through to deliver attacks on the American carriers. Had their skills been a bit sharper, especially in delivering torpedo attacks that had been deadly to USN carriers

An aviator from VT-28 aboard light carrier *Monterey* relaxes in his ready room after returning from the June 20 strike. VT-28 sent four Avengers on the mission and lost one to operational causes. Note the instruction on the ready room chalkboard to "Get the Carriers." (Naval History and Heritage Command)

An aviator from VT-28 aboard light carrier *Monterey* tells his buddies about his rescue at the hands of a destroyer three days after the June 20 strike on the First Mobile Fleet. Even though 209 American aircrew went missing after the strike, all but 49 were rescued in the days to follow. (Naval History and Heritage Command)

in 1942, the cost to the Americans would have been higher, but the outcome of the battle was never in doubt. In June 1944, the Japanese were unaware of the USN's use of radar-directed CAP that doomed large-scale attacks coming

Officers and crewmen on *Lexington* admire Japanese flags representing the 143 Japanese aircraft claimed by Air Group 16. Aside from one aircraft lost on June 19, Air Group 16 lost three to Japanese aircraft and another five to operational causes on June 20 – the lightest losses of a fleet carrier that saw action on both days of the battle. (Naval History and Heritage Command)

in at high altitudes. One area of strength for the IJN was its superior search capabilities. Following the defeat at Midway, the Japanese had taken the importance of developing a strong search capability to heart. One area of weakness that became a major factor in the battle was the IJN's immature antisubmarine capability.

Ozawa fought an intelligent battle. He correctly assessed that Spruance was a cautious commander who would not venture far from Saipan. He used this insight to launch a number of carrier air strikes that would have been fatal to an American carrier task force by the standards of 1942. The overriding problem for Ozawa was that his aviators were nowhere near as skilled as earlier in the war. However skillfully Ozawa handled his fleet, he lacked the airpower to deal serious blows to TF 58. If Ozawa can be faulted for any errors in judgment during the battle, it was that he too readily believed the gross overestimation of success by Japanese aviators that led him to plan to continue a battle which was already lost.

SPRUANCE'S PERFORMANCE

Spruance's performance during the battle can be faulted in a number of areas. He was outmaneuvered by Ozawa and was never able to bring his overwhelming force fully to bear. He had convinced himself that the Japanese would attempt to draw him to the west and then conduct a flanking attack on the amphibious force off Saipan. He had good reason to think this since it was a fundamental aspect of the captured Z Plan and the pattern of Japanese movement on June 17–18 may have suggested to Spruance that Ozawa was shadowing TF 58 and possibly preparing a thrust from the south. However, Spruance assessed Japanese intentions incorrectly since Ozawa's real intention was to focus his attack on TF 58.

Spruance's decision not to move to the west on the night of June 18–19 was the most important of the battle since it shaped the type of battle that unfolded and limited the prospects for the USN to inflict an even more crippling defeat on the IJN. Spruance placed paramount importance on the security of the amphibious operation against Saipan. Tactically, on the night of June 18–19, he had a very incomplete picture of Japanese fleet strength and movements. What he did know at the time only served to convince him that the Japanese were preparing to split their forces and conduct an attack on the invasion force. He was convinced that the Japanese were after the transports and not Mitscher's carriers.

The plan that Spruance settled on could have been disastrous. He was content to expose his carriers to attack without any real prospect of hitting back at Ozawa's carriers. At no other carrier battle of the war had a commander taken such an approach. Only the marked disparity between the skill of American and Japanese aviators prevented this strategy from backfiring. Spruance understood his aviators were better, but nobody could have foreseen that Japanese aviators would be totally ineffective in the attacks of June 19. Only good fortune prevented a much greater level of damage to TF 58.

Spruance's fear that the Japanese could slip around TF 58 and attack the invasion force was grossly misplaced. The invasion force was moved to safety 200 miles east of Saipan when the battle began. Even after

Spruance reinforced TF 58's screen with combatants from the invasion force, significant USN forces remained to protect the beachhead. It was unlikely that the Japanese were going to be able to conduct a flanking attack against the invasion force in the face of Mitscher's carrier force with its overwhelming striking power and ability to scout large swaths of ocean.

Spruance seemed to be thinking as a surface warfare officer, which he was. In carrier warfare, it was unlikely that an attacker could successfully perform a flanking maneuver.

Spruance was aware of the poor state of IJN carrier aviation training. This may have underpinned his willingness to expose his carriers to attack, but it should also have informed his opinion of how ineffective they could also be against the invasion fleet. The Japanese fuel situation was generally known to the Americans and that should have also made them think an end run was not only unlikely, but logistically impossible. And had the Japanese actually maneuvered with the intent to reach the beachhead, the result would have been a pyrrhic victory at best. With the invasion force moved well to the east of Saipan, all that was left exposed were a few LSTs whose loss would have been insignificant. After attacking the invasion force, the First Mobile Fleet would likely have been in a position with TF 58 to its west, making escape difficult and bringing the overwhelming striking power of Mitscher's carriers into full play. The results would have been truly decisive, and any IJN cripples would not have been able to escape. Spruance fought the conservative battle Ozawa knew he would, which meant that the Americans won the battle in spite of poor command decisions. The American victory was due to superior fighter interception doctrine and better-trained aviators.

In the final analysis, Spruance was unable to bring the full power of the USN into play, and missed a golden opportunity to not only cripple the IJN's carrier aviation force, but also destroy the last of its carriers. Perhaps this misses the central point. The results of the battle were decisive. The

Following the battle of Philippine Sea, the Fast Carrier Task Force, now redesignated TF 38 and part of the Third Fleet, went on to support the invasion of the Philippines in October. During this period, it defeated the IJN's last major operation at the battle of Leyte Gulf and contended with a constant threat of Japanese land-based aircraft, which included the first use of suicide aircraft. This is TF 38 at anchor in Ulithi Atoll on December 8, 1944 during a break from operations in the Philippines area. The carriers are (from front to back): *Wasp*, *Yorktown*, *Hornet*, *Hancock* and *Ticonderoga*. All are painted in the various dazzle camouflage schemes. (Naval History and Heritage Command)

IJN's carrier force was eliminated as a factor for the remainder of the war. The fact that six of Ozawa's carriers escaped with empty decks was of little consequence.

Nevertheless, the impact of Philippine Sea shaped the next great naval battle of the war. In October 1944, the Americans invaded the island of Leyte in the Philippines. The lack of a functional carrier force made the Japanese devise a desperate plan in which their remaining carriers, carrying the equivalent number of aircraft to a single Essex-class carrier, were to be sacrificed to draw the USN's Fast Carrier Task Force away from the invasion beachhead. Once lured away, the Japanese intended to attack the beachhead with a large force of battleships and heavy cruisers. To avoid the disappointment of the battle of the Philippine Sea from occurring again, for the Leyte invasion Nimitz gave explicit orders that if the Japanese fleet appeared its destruction was the prime objective. These orders were issued to an entirely different type of admiral known for being aggressive to the point of impulsiveness. When William Halsey received reports of the Japanese carriers, he immediately went after them with his entire force, setting up the most controversial naval drama of the Pacific War.

The final legacy of Philippine Sea was that it clearly demonstrated to key leaders in the IJN that there was no future in conventional air attacks against the USN. The solution was the adoption of suicide attacks that began at Leyte Gulf and continued in increasing ferocity until the end of the war. This was brought to an end by the employment of the atomic bomb against Japan. This operation originated from an airfield in the Marianas, the final legacy of the battle of the Philippine Sea.

BIBLIOGRAPHY

Buell, Thomas B., *The Quiet Warrior: A Biography of Admiral Raymond A. Spruance*, Naval Institute Press: Annapolis, Maryland (1987)

Dickson, W. D., *The Battle of the Philippine Sea*, Ian Allan: London (1975)

Dull, Paul S., *A Battle History of the Imperial Japanese Navy (1941–1945)*, Naval Institute Press: Annapolis, Maryland (1978)

Foreign Histories Division, General Headquarters Far East Command, *Japanese Monograph No. 90, The "A-Go" Operations May–June 1944*, Tokyo (1950)

Foreign Histories Division, General Headquarters Far East Command, *Japanese Monograph No. 91, The "A-Go" Operations Log Supplement: May–June 1944*, Tokyo (1950)

Foreign Histories Division, General Headquarters Far East Command, *Japanese Monograph No. 117, Outline of Third Phase Operations (February 1943 to August 1945)*, Tokyo (1950)

Foreign Histories Division, General Headquarters Far East Command, *Japanese Monograph No. 184, Submarine Operations in the Third Phase Operations*, Tokyo (1950)

Grove, Eric, *Fleet to Fleet Encounters*, Arms and Armour: London (1991)

Kawasaki, Manabu, *A New View of the Battle of Philippine Sea*, Dainihon Kaiga: Tokyo (2007)

Morison, Samuel Eliot, *History of United States Naval Operations in World War II, Volume VIII, New Guinea and the Marianas March 1944–August 1944*, Little, Brown and Company: Boston (1975)

Reynolds, Clark, *The Fast Carriers*, Naval Institute Press, Annapolis: Maryland (1992)

Tillman, Barrett, *Clash of the Carriers*, NAL Caliber: New York (2005)

United States Fleet, *Battle Experience: Supporting Operations for the Capture of the Marianas Islands (Saipan Guam and Tinian) June August 1944* (1944)

Vego, Milan, *Major Fleet-versus-Fleet Operations in the Pacific War, 1941–1945*, Naval War College Press: Newport, Rhode Island (2014)

www.combinedfleet.com

Y'Blood, William T., *Red Sun Setting*, Naval Institute Press: Annapolis, Maryland (1981)

INDEX